The Essence and Implications of *Missio Dei*

An appraisal of today's foremost theology of missions

The Essence and Implications of *Missio Dei*

An appraisal of today's foremost theology of missions

P. Pikkert

alev books

ALEV Books
168 Cornwallis Road
Ancaster, ON
Canada L9C 4H3
www.alevbooks.com

ISBN: 978-0-9881252-9-2

Layout by ALEVBOOKS
Garamond 11.5/24
Printed in the USA, United Kingdom and Germany by CreateSpace.

Keywords: missio Dei, missions, Christian missions, theology of missions.

Author's webpage: www.pikkert.com

For my many friends and colleagues in

WEC International

Contents

Preface

♦ ♦ ♦

THE TERM *missio Dei*, Latin for 'the mission of God', has been used by the church for centuries. Within current missiological thinking, however, it refers to a particular theology of Christian mission which has become the most widely accepted framework within which the enterprise is conceived today.

Missio Dei is not a well-defined theology. Its presence in contemporary missions is very tangible yet grasping it can be a frustrating endeavor. Every time you think you have managed it you are introduced to another perspective or alternative variant. Some now speak of "theologies of *missio Dei*". In order to respond to it, however, we must seek to grasp its essential features.

In its simplest form *missio Dei* means that "mission is God's, not ours" (Potter 1981:74). No Christian questions the fact that mission has its origins in God. Since the 1950s, however, that idea was conceptualized in new and different ways which would have far-reaching implications—so much so that it came to be called "a Copernican revolution in understanding the mission of the church" (Ott 2016:xiv).

This book seeks to identify the main contours of *missio Dei*, trace its trajectories and express some concerns. It started out as a position paper for Cornerstone, a Christian college run by WEC International in The Netherlands. That original paper triggered extensive feedback ranging from high praise to the highly critical. Pleasant as the praise was, the critical voices were much more helpful, for their input highlighted weaknesses in that original paper and resulted in this revision.

One of the concerns pointed out by the critics was that people of otherwise very different theological persuasions ended up sharing the same platform. In other words, evangelicals who are critical of the liberal versions of *missio Dei's* marginalizaton of substitutionary atonement, of the need for evangelism, and of the role of the church, can end up looking as if they are closely linked to those views. They are not, and I have tried hard to distinguish between them. However, I could not fully resolve the issue; it is an almost inescapable problem in short works on sweeping movements—and few theological movements are as broadly accepted ecumenically and as wide-ranging as *missio Dei.* From chapter four onwards the book focuses mainly on the way the concept has been defined by David Bosch, Christopher Wright and, to a lesser extent, Scott Sunquist as these men have been very instrumental in shaping current evangelical thinking on the subject.

A closely associated problem arose from the fact that I tried to present *missio Dei* as fairly as possible by letting its major proponents speak for themselves. The problem with this is that quotations have contexts. It is all too easy to string together carefully chosen quotes from a variety of sources and end up creating a false impression, an unfair interpretation, or an unwarranted extension of meaning. In long, thoughtful letters both Birgit Herppich of my own mission, WEC International, and Christopher Wright identified a number of places where they thought I fell into that trap. I have tried to correct any unfair extrapolations to the best of my ability without turning this into a tome. Nevertheless, a reductionist element in a work this short is unavoidable, and I advise readers who want to pursue this subject further to read the works of the writers quoted.

The book is structured as follows: Chapter 1 looks at *missio Dei*'s main tenets. Chapter 2 takes a brief look at the emergence of the original model in the wake of the Second World War and its subsequent near-collapse as a Christian formulation of missions. Chapter 3 traces the development of the evangelical version of the model, and Chapter 4 looks at the supporting hermeneutic. Chapter 5 reviews the model's critiques of the older, salvation-orientated theology of missions it seeks to replace, and Chapter 6 delves into problems with respect to some of the model's propositions. In Chapter 7 I present the contours of an alternative vision for Christian missionary theology.

I thank Dr. George Bristow, Rev. Carl Muller and my son Owen Pikkert for their input. I am particularly grateful to my colleague Martin Till, the dean here at Cornerstone, for encouraging me to pursue this project and for his insights along the way. I am most thankful for Drs. Birgit Herppich and Christopher Wright's gracious critiques. As Dr. Wright concluded in his letter, "doubtless we shall continue to disagree! Hopefully we can sustain the spirit of Romans 14-15 in the midst of disagreement, and continue to uphold the great missional truths and imperatives of the scriptures!" Amen to that.

I hope and pray that this little book, imperfect though it is, will contribute to the ongoing debate on the historical and theological foundation of the Christian missionary enterprise, and in doing so help clarify thinking and mission praxis on this important subject.

Peter Pikkert
Cornerstone College for Mission Training, 2017

1

What is *Missio Dei*?

♦ ♦ ♦

THE CONCEPT of *missio Dei* has led two lives. It was first embraced by the mainline, conciliar churches. When it had virtually run its course there a number of theologically more conservative missiologists embraced the basic idea, reconceptualized aspects of it, and saw it become the most popular theological basis for missions.

The earlier confessional approach embraced a more "world-focused" model in which God was perceived as working actively in every sphere of life. This led to the marginalization of the role of the church in missions, to the idea that "it could be mentioned only in passing and without strong emphasis" (Engelsviken 2003:488). Those with more conservative theological convictions continued to see God working through the church, though not exclusively so. The following basic concepts are broadly accepted by almost all adherents of *missio Dei*.

1.1. Christian mission is the all-encompassing work of the Triune God

The fundamental idea of *missio Dei* is that Christian mission is rooted in the Trinitarian nature of God: "Evangelism is God's work long before it is our work. The Father prepares the ground, the Son gives the invitation and the Spirit prompts the person to respond in repentance and faith to the good news" (Kirk 1999:78). David Bosch, who played a seminal role in the formulation and promotion of *missio Dei*, and whose work on the subject is embraced by both its evangelical and ecumenical adherents, states that Christian mission must be "put in the context of the doctrine of the Trinity, not of ecclesiology or soteriology… Mission is, primarily and ultimately, the work of the triune God, Creator, Redeemer, and Sanctifier, for the sake of the world" (Bosch 1991:390-391).

This focus on Christian mission as the all-encompassing work of the triune God led to a shift in focus from missions as something which the church does to something which God Himself does directly using various and sundry ways and means.

> To say that the church is essentially missionary does not mean that mission is church-centered. It is *missio Dei.* It is Trinitarian. It is mediating the love of God the Father who is the Parent of all people, whoever and wherever they may be. It is epiphany, the making present in the world of God the Son. It is mediating the presence of God the Spirit, who blows where he wishes, without us knowing whence he comes and whither he goes (Jn. 3:8) (Bosch 1991:505).

Lesslie Newbigin, an early exponent of the model, holds that God's missionary enterprise cannot be properly understood "except within the framework of a fully and explicitly trinitarian doctrine of God" (Newbigin 1964:31).

> Mission is not just something that the church does; it is something that is done by the Spirit, who is himself the witness, who changes both the world and the church, who always goes before the church on its missionary journey (Newbigin 1995:132).

The German missiologist Georg F. Vicedom, a major proponent of *missio Dei* during the 1950s and 1960s, drew the following conclusions:

> The mission is work that belongs to God. This is the first implication of *missio Dei.* God is the Lord, the One who gives the orders, the Owner, the One who takes care of things. He is the Protagonist in the mission. When we ascribe the mission to God in this way, then it is withdrawn from human whims (Vicedom 1965:5).

1.2. God's mission flows from His loving and compassionate nature

Virtually all advocates of *missio Dei*, whether Evangelical, Conciliar or Roman Catholic, perceive God's love as his defining characteristic, their descriptions of the divine attribute sometimes rising to soaring heights. David Bosch wrote: "God is a fountain of sending love. This is the deepest source of mission. It is impossible to penetrate deeper still; there is mission because God loves people" (Bosch 1991:402, also 1980:240). He echoes an earlier statement issued by the Roman Catholic Church during Vatican II:

> This plan [*missio Dei*] flows from the 'fountain-like love' of God the Father. As the principle without principle from whom the Son is generated and from whom the Holy Spirit proceeds through the Son, God in his great and merciful kindness... never ceases to pour out his divine goodness (*Ad Gentes* 1965:814, quoted in Thomas 1996:90).

The evangelicals agree. Orlando Costas affirms that "love is the foundation of God's existence" (Costas 1989:74); "God's compassion and love for his creation is his paramount, even overwhelming, attribute" (Guder 1998:32; Kirk 1999:27).

> To summarize: in both the Old and New Testaments God reveals himself as the One who has compassion on the less privileged, the marginal figures, and the outcasts. He is the God of grace. If we look for a biblical foundation for mission we will find it in this essential element of biblical religion as a religion of mercy and compassion... A religion in which compassion occupies so central a position, cannot but be a missionary religion (Bosch 1980:57).

1.3. God's mission encompasses all of human life

One of David Bosch's simpler formulations of *missio Dei* is "God's involvement in and with the world, the nature and activity of God, which embraces both the church and the world, and in which the church is privileged to participate. *Missio Dei* enunciates the good news that God is a God-for-people" (Bosch 1991:10). Bosch here clearly states the concept's wholistic embrace, a fundamental idea all *missio Dei* proponents share. Johannes Hoekendijk, representing the conciliar branch of the church, referred to it as "the entirety of God's action which is focussed upon the sharing of the messianic way of life with people, so that, in the perspective of Shalom, the horizons of hope are opened up for us all" (Hoekendijk quoted in Thomas 1996:126-127).

Johannes Verkuyl, formerly professor of missiology and evangelism at the Free University of Amsterdam, believes that God is "actively engaged in the reestablishment of His liberating dominion over the cosmos and all of humankind" (Verkuyl 1993:72). Emilio Castro, formerly General Secretary of the World Council of Churches, holds that "the purpose of God is... to gather the whole of creation under the Lordship of Christ Jesus in whom, by the power of the Holy Spirit, all are brought into communion with God" (Castro 1993:133).

The evangelicals concur. Wilbert Shenk, senior professor of mission history at Fuller, notes that "the redemptive power of God is now being guided by a particular strategy in order to bring the divine purpose to completion by delivering the creation from the powers of decay and death" (Shenk 1996:84). Orlando Costas states that

> Contextual evangelization implies witnessing everywhere and at all times in the presence of the total activity of the triune God... This implies that we cannot separate God's redemptive activities in the evangelistic process from what Father, Son and Spirit are doing in the secular affairs of life. The same God who created the world redeemed it. The same God who provides for the well-being of the earth judges those who exploit and destroy its resources... Communicating the good news of salvation with integrity in our respective life situations means relating that message to God's involvement in all spheres of human life and to the totality of God's concern for the well-being of our planet and the universe (Costas 1989:84).

Christopher Wright, of whom we will hear much more, states that "the fact is that sin and evil constitute bad news in every area of life on this planet. The redemptive work of God through the cross of Christ is good news for every area of life on earth that has been touched by sin. Bluntly, we need a holistic gospel because the world is in a holistic mess" (Wright 2006:315).

This leads us to the next point: what, exactly, does this all-encompassing plan which the Triune God is conceived as accomplishing actually involve? What is its goal, its purpose?

1.4. The goal of God's mission: the restoration of creation

The goal toward which God's all-embracing love drives him is, as a song currently popular puts it, to "make all things right". In other words, as creator of the world, God's salvific purposes are not limited to the salvation of souls but extends to the establishment of a new "shalom" in the here and now: "The goal towards which God is working, the ultimate end of his mission, is the establishment of shalom. This involves the realization of the full potentialities of all creation and its ultimate reconciliation and unity in Christ" (Potter 1981:70-74).

This restoration is perceived as taking place — at least in large part — in the current historical reality. Mission thus seeks to utilize historic processes as it seeks to transform the world into the kingdom of God. Herewith a few sample affirmations:

> We cannot separate God's redemptive activities in the evangelistic process from what Father, Son and Spirit are doing in the secular affairs of life... Communicating the good news of salvation with integrity in our respective life situations means relating that message to God's involvement in all the spheres of human life and to the totality of God's concern for the well-being of our planet and the universe (Costas 1989:84).

> [God] wants to let the human race be whole again and no longer *homines religionis*, who after all, are still fettered in their chains. At the cross and at the resurrection, there was made a beginning of this humanizing process, and it is working in culture as fermentation. Where a liberation to a rightful humanization is taking place, one can conclude that the *missio Dei*, once again, has reached its goal (Thomas 1996:126).

Christopher Wright, linking the Bible's eschatological vision of a restored creation with missionary activity in the here-and-now states that:

> The mission of God is ultimately to restore his whole creation to what it was intended to be — God's creation, ruled over by redeemed humanity, giving glory and praise to its creator. Our mission, in participation with that divine mission, and in anticipation of its final accomplishment, is to work with God in exposing the idols that continue to blur the distinction, and to liberate men and women from the destructive delusions they foster (Wright 2006:165).

These destructive delusions include all the idols, evils, false hopes and enticements of Western culture, ranging from material prosperity to "New-age-ism, narcissism and hedonism" (2006:166).

1.5. The church is invited to be a participant with God in His mission

In the triune God's mission of global restoration/transformation He invites the church to participate in what He is doing. In other words, mission is not perceived primarily as an activity of the church, but as flowing directly from God in which the church is invited to participate. The German theologian Jürgen Moltmann phrased it as follows: "It is not the church that has a mission of salvation to fulfill in the world; it is the mission of the Son and the Spirit through the Father that includes the church" (Moltmann 1977:64).

The idea of the church as a participant of one of many means which God uses in his project of establishing "shalom" is strongly and repeatedly affirmed: "The *missio Dei* is God's activity, which embraces both the church and the world, and in which the church may be privileged to participate" (Bosch 1991:401).

> It cannot be denied that the *missio Dei* notion has helped to articulate the conviction that neither the church nor any other human agent can ever be considered the author or bearer of mission. Mission is, primarily and ultimately, the work of the Triune God, Creator, Redeemer, and Sanctifier, for the sake of the world, a ministry in which the church is privileged to participate (Bosch 1991:302).

The nature of the church's actual role in God's program is variously described, depending on the particular author's theological perceptions. Moltmann states that "what we have to learn is not that the church 'has' a mission, but the very reverse: that the mission of Christ creates its own church… Mission does not come from the church". The church is merely "one element in the movements of the divine sending, gathering together, and experience" (Moltmann 1977:64-65). In the 1960s the Dutch missiologist Johannes C. Hoekendijk "was almost savage in his denunciation of the illegitimacy of a church-centered approach to the missionary task" (Glasser & McGavan 1983:93). His insistence on making the concerns of the world the focus of concern for the church led the World Council of Churches to adopt the watchword "the world sets the agenda of the church" because it is called to serve it" (Ott 2016:xv).

Thankfully, not everyone is that extreme. Christopher Wright, an evangelical, maintains that "fundamentally, our mission… means our committed participation as God's people, at God's invitation and command, in God's own mission within the history of God's world for the redemption of God's creation" (Wright 2006:23). In short, the church's job is to participate in what God is already doing globally.

> *Mission is not ours; mission is God's.* Certainly, the mission of God is the prior reality out of which flows any mission that we get involved in. Or, as has been nicely put, it is not so much the case that God has a mission for his church in the world but that God has a church for his mission in the world. Mission was not made for the church; the church was made for mission—God's mission (italics in original, 2006:62).

For his part, Scott Sunquist, currently dean of Fuller's School of Intercultural Studies, eloquently describes *missio Dei* as follows: "*Missio Dei* must be understood as a foundational concept that launches the church from the place of worship and fellowship into the frontiers of God's reign. Living such a life, participating with God in such a movement, is costly and painful, and yet, in the end, it is glorious" (Sunquist 2013:xiii).

♦ ♦ ♦

How can one possibly disapprove of a wholistic theology of missions which has its roots in the love of the triune God who invites his people to join him in the restoration of all things? Criticising such a broadly accepted, God-centered theological position rings of petty narrow-mindedness, of reflecting the sentiments of some bigoted, by-gone era which the church, including evangelicals, are thought to have left behind: "It is inconceivable that we could again revert to a narrow, ecclesiocentric view of mission" (Bosch 1991:402).

There are, however, a numbers of questions which do not fit easily into the model:

- Are God's love and compassion really the divine attributes which trump all others? How do such attributes as divine holiness, and doctrines such as election fit into the model?
- What did Christ actually die for, and for whom did he do so?
- If everything God does is mission, then what is Christian mission? In other words, what is the specific role of the

church in contradistinction to every other positive and uplifting human activity?

- If *missio Dei* is everything God is doing in the cosmos does that include the idea of divine judgment within history, as well as the idea of eternal judgment?
- Does hell still factor as a motive for missions? Are sinners still perceived as hell-bound if they haven't personally accepted Christ's redeeming work at Calvary?
- How does the idea of evil as something which, at times at least, is specifically allowed and used by God for soteriological purposes fit into the model?
- How do the Bible's teachings on spiritual warfare, the ongoing reality of evil, and the demonic fit into the model?
- Is God even interested in transforming this world, in making this particular world a better place? Or does the Bible teach that things will, in fact, go from bad to worse prior to Christ's second coming, and that the shalom-state of which the prophets spoke will not commence until then?

Questions of this nature were left largely unanswered by the original, mainline proponents of *missio Dei*. As more theologically conservative theologians and the evangelicals joined the conversation, however, attempts were made to integrate at least some of these concerns into the model.

2

The Emergence, Spread, and Near-Death of *Missio Dei*

♦ ♦ ♦

BEFORE WE describe the version of *missio Dei* so popular today we trace, as briefly as possible, the emergence, spread and evolution of the original concept. We place these developments in their social context because changes in worldviews, specific theologies included, do not emerge in a vacuum. We begin with the concept's trajectory within the mainline, conciliar churches where it had its roots.

Missio Dei, as a theological foundation for the missionary enterprise, first emerged at a popular level at the Willingen Conference of the International Missionary Council in 1952, where the delegates affirmed that "mission is derived from the very nature of God" (Thomas 1996:102). The Latin term describing the concept was coined several years later, as part of the title of Georg F. Vicedom's 1958 book *Missio Dei: Einführung in eine Theologie der Mission* ("Missio Dei: Introduction to a Theology of Mission") (see Rosin 1972:8).

The world in 1952 had changed radically since, say, the optimistic Edinburgh conference of 1910 which had met under the banner of "The Evangelization of the World in This Generation". Numerous mission organizations folded in the wake of World War I, and the preoccupation of the majority of remaining missionaries — a fraction of their prewar number — was keeping the educational and medical institutions going in places where they had not been nationalized (Mott 1924:327-328). In Europe the war was followed by large-scale unemployment and hyper-inflation. Marxism and fascism became the secular faiths for most people, and the influence of the church on society became so negligible that neither the Church of England, nor the Lutheran and Catholic churches of Germany, nor the Russian Orthodox church were able to prevent the near suicide of the continent. In North America neither the general prosperity and cultural ferment of the 1920s, nor the depression of the 1930s led to a resurgence in missionary interest because isolationist tendencies had turned the continent inward. The immediate post-WWII period was no better. Europe, devastated once again, was in no position to send missionaries. The mainline churches of America did not do so either. Haunted by the depression and the war, people settled down and, though very active religiously, were not ready to launch new ambitious ventures. "What was wanted was for the church to be a rock, not Peter's barque setting out for new shores" (Ellwood 2000:5).

The problem was, however, much greater than the physical collapse of the missionary enterprise. The root of the crisis was theological. The theological foundations on which the missionary enterprise of the latter half of the 19th century had been based proved to be largely bankrupt. In the course of the 19th century the application of historical and literary criticism and the liberal theologies of Friedrich Schleiermacher, David F. Strauss and Albrecht Ritschl had created tremendous ferment, which led to strongly critical attitudes towards the idea of Christian mission. Subsequent opinions of what Christian mission ought to look like polarized into "Liberal" and "Conservative-evangelical" groups, with the Liberal wing focusing on social action: "we must be willing to give without any preaching" (Hocking 1932:70).

Furthermore, post-millennialism — one of the main theological underpinnings of the 19th century's more conservative missionaries — died in the trenches of the Great War. Ideas about the uniqueness of the Christian religion, faith in a loving and benevolent God, and notions about the superiority of Western civilization which, when influenced by Christianity, would inevitably lead to progress died with it. By the late 1940s the missionary movement of the mainline churches was in a state of crisis; the first post-war ecumenical missions conference, Whitby 1947, took place in an "atmosphere of embarrassment" (Bosch 1980:175). A major new impulse was needed.

Missio Dei proved to be that new, rejuvenating impulse and, as such, was eagerly embraced by the mainline churches. Interestingly, at a grass-roots level it allowed them to continue "doing missions" in much the same way as before. The foundation had changed, but it fit their existing superstructure which, by then, consisted by-and-large of sponsoring educational and medical institutions.

During the 1960s and 70s various liberation theologians also came to embrace *missio Dei.* No wonder: the idea that everything that is good, that is liberating, is part of God's mission provided a ready theological basis for their concerns. In fact, a case can be made that the various liberation theologies are not so much descendants of the old German liberal theology as of *missio Dei.* They certainly cross-fertilized: "liberation theologies have given precise content to the secularized *missio Dei* of the sixties with its questionable assertion that relating to anything one thinks God is doing in the world today is the church's 'mission'. Liberation theologies have transformed *missio Dei* into politics" (Glasser & McGavran 1983:165).

> *Missio Dei* became a neologism that blurred God's providential governance over the nations with the church's mission. Radical formulations came to the fore until *missio Dei* was so reinterpreted and modified that it came to mean the action of God in carrying out His judgments and His ameliorating work among the nations in the revolutionary movements of our day (1983:92).

As a result the church's mission was secularized and the idea of missions as confrontation, as proclamation, as a call to repentance and faith withered and died. After all, the "activity of God was to be found in all those movements leading to the humanization of individuals and society" (1983:93).

The Dutch missiologist and theologian Libertus Hoedemaker also began to question the usefulness of the *missio Dei* model, warning that it "could be used by people who subscribe to mutually exclusive theological positions" (quoted in Bosch 1991:392). Lesslie Newbigin, director of the World Council of Churches' Commission on World Mission during the early 1960s, and an early proponent of the model, came to recognizing that the phrase *"missio Dei"*

> was sometimes used in such a way as to marginalize the role of the church. If God is indeed the true missionary, it was said, our business is not to promote the mission of the church, but to get out into the world, find out "what God is doing in the world," and join forces with him. And "what God is doing" was generally thought to be in the secular rather than in the religious sectors of human life. The effect, of course, was to look for what seemed to be the rising powers and to identify Christian missionary responsibility with support for a range of political and cultural developments, sometimes bizarre indeed (Newbigin 1995:18).

David Bosch, for his part, noted approvingly that missions consisted of "God's turning to the world in respect of creation, care, redemption and consummation. It takes place in ordinary human history, not exclusively in and through the church" (Bosch 1992:390). Bosch also recognized the inherent danger that those "who supported the wider understanding of the concept tended to radicalize the view that the *missio Dei* was larger than the mission of the church, even to the point of suggesting that it excluded the church's involvement" (1992:392).

If God's mission was everything God was doing, if, in fact, the church itself was an object of God's mission, it is no wonder that the Christian missionary enterprise declined in the mainline churches. "Because of the basic changes in the understanding of mission precipitated by the re-conceptualization of *missio Dei*, the missionary involvement of churches within the conciliar movement went almost immediately into sharp decline" (Glasser & McGavran 1983:95).

As the role of the church in God's mission within the mainline, conciliar churches secularized and virtually disappeared the original version of *missio Dei* suffered a near-death experience as a genuinely Christian formulation of the church's missionary mandate.

3

Missio Dei Resurrected by Theological Conservatives and Evangelicals

♦ ♦ ♦

IN THE 1950s and 60s American evangelicalism was emerging from the traumatic modernist-fundamentalist wars of the inter-war period to become a significant new socio-political force. Its intellectual center was Fuller Theological Seminary, in California. Unlike the old fundamentalism, the new evangelicalism was tolerant in non-essentials, well informed with respect to science and culture, able and willing to both examine itself and accept social responsibility, and "serious about building a rational philosophical foundation for traditional Christianity" (Ellwood 2000:186). It became the 'quintessential American religion' an inter-denominational mass cultural movement birthing numerous para-church organizations, from which a fresh push for global missions emerged (:185, :194). This transformation of evangelicalism, taking place when all other mainline Christian streams were stagnant and in decline (Johnstone 1978:27), gained the initiative in the church worldwide, resulting in a large cohort of conservative evangelical baby boomers forming the backbone of the missionary enterprise during the 1970s and 80s.

The new evangelicalism's theology had tremendous motivational power, even if it was considered simplistic and one-dimensional by mainline church missionaries. One of its defining characteristics was that the 'gospel message' was supra-cultural. Certain key doctrines and terms (inspiration of Scripture, atonement, redemption in Christ, repentance, personal faith, regeneration, heaven, hell) which comprise the gospel "are not cultural but transcendent, standing above all cultures in judgement and with a call to individuals to come out of the world to eternal salvation" (Ellwood 2000:191). Their missionary movement focused on church planting, and "enshrines basic facts of the Christian gospel which are never lost sight of" (Douglas 1966:423).

However, change was in the wind. At the 1974 International Congress on World Evangelism in Lausanne, Switzerland, Samuel Escobar pushed for a more wholistic attitude in Christian missions. Together with René Padilla he warned against the presentation of a gospel which made no social, political and economic demands. In doing so they secured the Lausanne Covenant affirmation that "evangelism and socio-political involvement are both part of our Christian duty". Its 'Section 5: Social Responsibility' states:

> We therefore should share his (i.e. God's) concern for justice and reconciliation throughout human society and for the liberation of men and women from every kind of oppression. Because men and women are made in the image of God, every person, regardless of race, religion, colour, culture, class, sex or age, has an intrinsic dignity because of which he or she should be respected and served, not exploited… We affirm that evangelism and socio-political involvement are both part of our Christian duty.

Under the influence of these early 'left wing' evangelical leaders evangelicalism took a major step in the direction of a more wholistic understanding of mission, one which would come to typify the somewhat later evangelical expression of *missio Dei.*

Many of the older generation of evangelical theologians, missionaries and missiologists (people like Herbert Kane, Donald McGavran, Arthus Glasser, Ralph Winter, and the German Lutheran Peter Beyerhaus) were strongly suspicious of anything that smacked of *missio Dei.* Donald McGavran stated his fears and concerns in clear terms:

> In time the major implications of this reconceptualization of *missio Dei* began to filter down to the churches. In all too many circles they came as heady wine. There was no longer any reason for the church to confront the world with a message whose first word was 'Repent!' There was no essential difference between Christians and non-Christians. The significant activity of God was to be found in all those movements leading to the humanization of individuals and

> society. Working for the conversion of non-Christians was passé (Glasser & McGavran 1983:93).

That generation fought a losing battle. As we will see, major aspects of the "old-time gospel" of the conservative evangelicals were lost sight of, as a reformulated, evangelical version of *missio Dei* swept up the new generation of postmodern, GenX missionaries, whose mindset was more amenable to a more wholistic approach to the 'big questions' facing modern man than their Boomer predecessors.

> Post-modernity calls us back to a more holistic and community-based understanding of what it means to be human, and post-modern Christians have enthusiastically welcomed this return to scriptural values. In turn, post-modern Christians, missionaries included, are likely to be more concerned with moral issues such as weapons of mass destruction, environmental destruction, women's rights, Third World debt, racism, exploitation of child labor, and so on (Tiplady 2002:23).

Unlike their Boomer predecessors, many GenXers were also theologically fuzzy (Borthwick 2003:438), something compounded by the virtue of tolerance, which "often belies an implicit theological pluralism" (:440). This meant that evangelical mission agencies began accepting large numbers of young people with sharp social consciences but with weakened theological convictions. When some theologically more conservative scholars rescued *missio Dei* from the liberation theologians, an entire generation of missionaries, already at odds with their Boomer predecessors over many things, were ready to buy into it. When they eventually went to beef up their theological education they would go to schools which were formerly bastions of the older theology, but which had, in the meantime, made radical theological shifts towards a modified form of *missio Dei.*

The person who, more than any other, facilitated this shift was the South African missiologist David J. Bosch. Basically Bosch provided empirical proof for the fact that models of missions change over time: "Precisely the historical character of biblical revelation is of essential significance for a biblical foundation of mission" (Bosch 1980:61). His concept of different paradigms of mission allowed the subject to be conceptualized as something which is constantly evolving, changing, morphing into forms appropriate for the time and context. This being the case, he draws the conclusion that the nature of missions can, and has, evolved according to the historical context.[1]

His monumental work, *Transforming Mission*, called "one of the 100 most significant books of the 20th century" by *Christianity Today* (see cover, 2011 edition), traces the various paradigms of missions he sees within the Bible and in the course of history. If missions is something which evolved, then the latest manifestation, *missio Dei*, could be perceived as the culmination of a historic development which has its roots in the history of Israel. Bosch also sought to wed a more theologically conservative position with the main basic tenets of *missio Dei*. This led him to give the person of Jesus Christ and the role of the church a higher priority than had hitherto been the case.

During the 1980s the "radical" evangelicals began to buy into *missio Dei* as well, particularly some of the Latin American evangelicals laboring in the same social context as their Roman Catholic liberation theologian counterparts, men such as René Padilla, Orlando Costas, and Samuel Escobar, who, as seen, had already been moving the church towards assuming greater social responsibility.[2]

We begin by describing the actual practices of the evangelical version of *missio Dei*, after which we will outline the hermeneutical principles on which the practices are based as presented by Christopher Wright. If this sequence seems counterintuitive (after all, praxis should follow the application of proper exegesis), that is because the development of the supportive hermeneutic came after the development of the "evangelical" version of *missio Dei*.

3.1. God's love and compassion remain the wellspring of God's mission

This is not a point we need to belabour. We have already quoted David Bosch, Andrew Kirk and Orlando Costas (see 1.2) on this

---

[1] Bosch's view of different paradigms in missions sounds a lot like Thomas Kuhn's views on the philosophy of science. Though within philosophy Kuhn's views are highly contested, they have been taken as gospel truth by many outside that discipline, distorted in ways he would not have accepted, and applied to areas he would not have accepted either.

[2] Interestingly, while Lausanne moved the evangelical world towards a more wholistic understanding of mission, the World Council of Churches began to rearticulate the importance of evangelism as core to missions. The focus of this book is on developments within the evangelical world.

fundamental conviction, one shared by virtually all the evangelical proponents of *missio Dei*. The application is clear: mission is about reflecting the unconditional, all-embracing love of God for the whole world.

3.2. God's mission retains its wholistic, comprehensive, transformational thrust

Christian mission continues to be perceived as a wholistic enterprise. Ronald Sider, a Mennonite, was an early proponent of this kind of wholistic comprehensiveness:

> Only if we biblical Christians throw ourselves into the struggle for social justice for the wretched of the earth so unequivocally that the poor and the oppressed know beyond all question that we will risk all in the struggle against economic and political oppression—only then will Third World theologians be willing to hear our critique of unbiblical definitions of salvation. And only then will the oppressed of the earth be able to hear our Good News about the risen Lord Jesus (Sider 1977:20).

A generation later Christopher Wright affirmed that "The totality of God's redemption includes all that God has done — from the exodus to the cross. It is not that the New Testament exchanges a social message for a spiritual one but that it extends the Old Testament teaching" (Wright 2006:279). As we will see when looking at missional hermeneutics, he makes much of the exodus as a paradigm for "comprehensive redemption" inasmuch as it touches on people's political, economic, social and spiritual lives (:268-271). In it "God responded to all the dimensions of Israel's need… It was God's total response to Israel's total need" (:271). As such, we should see it "in terms of release from slavery to all that oppresses human life and well-being and opposes God" (:278).

Chapter headings in *Mission as Transformation* (1999), edited by Samuel and Sugden of the Oxford Center of World Mission, speak for themselves: "Evangelical Christianity and the Environment," "A Christian Response to Population Issues," "Christian Relief and Development Agencies in the Twenty First Century," etc.

> The Christian faith stimulates us to look for the actualization of the kingdom in history in terms of justice, equal access to the creation that God intended for all, and the creation of

> human community through love, worship, work and play… Christians can invest their lives in the building of a historical order in the certainty that neither they nor their efforts are meaningless or lost (Samuel & Sugden 1999:189).

All this means that *missio Dei* remains a strong catalyst for church involvement in politics. According to Bosch "to argue that the Church should have nothing to do with politics is self-deception, not to get involved in politics means, in fact, to support the political status quo publicly or implicitly". He goes on to warn that the church should not "slip over into spiritualism, into a *dematerialization* and *de-politicization* of the Gospel" (italics in original, Bosch 1980:212, 226).

Wright seeks to strike a balance between political interpretations that omit the spiritual and evangelistic dimensions and spiritualized interpretations which ignore the social and political dimensions of life. Even when accompanied by evangelistic concerns, however, politicized interpretations lead to radical applications:

> For the church to get involved with issues of environmental protection it must be prepared to tackle the forces of greed and economic power, to confront vested interests and political machinations, to recognize that more is at stake than just being kind to animals and nice to people. It must do the scientific research to make its case credible. It must be willing for the long, hard road that the struggle for justice and compassion in a fallen world demands in this as in all other fields of mission (Wright 2006:417).

Here Wright's position does not appear to be essentially different from the radical priest Jean Marc Ella of a previous generation:

> the hope of a new world that is built in the framework of justice, peace, and freedom is the heart of the Christian message. We must get involved in this experience and use it as our starting-point for a radical critique of all that is happening before our eyes… The irruption of the poor throughout the countries of the Third World is radically changing the mission of the church… Our choice is simple: either we choose to work with the agents of change to create a world habitable for all, or we choose not to work with them (Ela 1988:91, 100).

3.3. The incarnation and suffering of Jesus Christ play multiple roles in the realization of God's mission

This is a tenet on which today's theologically conservative and evangelical advocates of *missio Dei* have a much sharper focus than many of their post WWII mainline predecessors: "Christocentric monotheism is profoundly missional, inasmuch as it says with equal strength… that YHWH is God in heaven above and the earth beneath, and there is no other; and that Jesus is Lord, and there is no other name under heaven given to humanity by which we must be saved" (Wright 2006:131).

The first reason that theological conservatives and evangelicals highlight the importance of Jesus Christ is the recognition that Christian mission can hardly be called "Christian" if there is no focus on what Christ has done:

> Mission is mission only if it aims at leading people to repentance and faith in Christ's finished work of redemption, if it seeks to incorporate those it reaches into the new Messianic community, and if it makes Christ's finished work of redemption relevant to the frontiers that are being crossed (Bosch 1993:441-442).

The frontiers which Christ's finished work needs to cross are, among others, described by Bosch as "ideological, cultural, religious, social, economic and ethnic" (:441).

Secondly, the incarnation is seen as demonstrating that God can and does work anywhere, and can do so directly: "The incarnation demonstrates that God's mission is not dependent on any one human culture or language" (Guder 2000:78).

Thirdly, Christ's self-sacrifice is presented as a demonstration of the depth of God's love:

> The cross shows a correspondence of wills between the Father and the Son: both act out of love and for love. Thus the cross discloses God's identity as the holy and loving Father and as the loving and obedient Son. There we see the Father passionately delivering the Son out of holy love for the world and the Son suffering death for the world in loving obedience to the Father (Costas 1989:75).

Fourthly, the incarnation and Christ's suffering is a model of how missions should be done and, as such, is perceived as being of great missiological importance: "In taking on human flesh of humanity and identifying himself with the poor, Jesus demonstrated where God's priorities lay, just as Jesus fulfilled his mission becoming poor (Richebacher 2003:594); "*Missio Dei* always leads us by way of Golgotha, by way of suffering" (Suess 2003:558). This idea is nicely communicated in the title of a book written by Scott Sunquist: *Understanding Christian Mission: Participation in Suffering and Glory* (2013). Quoting Moltmann, Sunquist points out that:

> It bears repeating that Moltmann identifies the church's missional reality in suffering. 'Participation in the apostolic mission of Christ therefore leads inescapably to tribulation, contradiction and suffering. The apostolate is carried out in the weakness and poverty of Christ, not through force or the strategies of force' (Sunquist 2013:278).

In short, "incarnational missionaries" are to enflesh the hopes, needs and aspirations of their host society as they imitate Christ's self-sacrificing love:

> The primary paradigm in Scripture for this approach to understanding mission is Jesus and his incarnation… Mission is to be incarnational ('go and be' among people) rather than attractional ('come to our meeting and see'). The end result of mission is not just conversion, nor just growing a church larger nor just planting new churches, but transformation—of individuals, communities and societies. Sometimes this is expressed as impacting the community for Christ, or 'building the kingdom', or helping create 'shalom' (Vanderwerf 2011:5).

We will return to the subject of the incarnational model of missions later.

Fifthly, Jesus Christ's role in God's mission is to restore the world to its rightful owner, God. Wright states that Jesus' role was: "to restore Israel to YHWH and also to be the agent of God's salvation reaching the ends of the earth" (Wright 2006:65). Sunquist sums this up neatly as well: "The same Word who created all things is the Word who became incarnate in Jesus Christ. So the renewal of creation is accomplished by the same word who created in the beginning" (Sunquist 2013:186).

3.4. The church regains a special role as a participant with God in his mission

In the evangelical model of *missio Dei* the church regains a place in mission:

> Christ is Head of both Church and cosmos, yet only in the Church is his headship acknowledged and confessed. The world has no faith to confess. It can neither pray nor believe. It cannot enter into a personal relationship with God. The Church is that segment of the world which submits consciously to Christ, obeys and serves him, albeit haltingly and with a stammer (Bosch 1980:221-222).

How the church's actual role is conceived varies widely. Wright argues strongly in both *The Mission of God* (2006) and in *The Mission of God's People* (2010) that the church have a powerful voice in all affairs of life, calling on it to "purge and redeem" the "public square" (Wright 2010:227). Others make much of the idea of a Christian "presence", an idea based on such verses as 1 Peter 2:12 and 2 Cor. 2:14 in which "Christians do not themselves publicize their faith… Wherever the apostle lives as 'Christ-fragrance', something happens to the surrounding people" (Bosch 1993:451).

> The message of this dumb and blind witness [referring to the servant of the Lord in Isaiah 42:18-20; 48:8-13] does not consist in verbal proclamation but that merely by his existence and his experience he is a witness for Yahweh. His mission consists in his being there for others (:445).

3.5. Other religious traditions must be treated with respect

God is perceived as glorying in cultural diversity. As we will see in the next section, this is drawn from the creation mandate and the fact that all men are created in God's image: "God glories in the diversity of cultures: this is seen in the affirmation of a specific culture in the incarnation, in the Scriptures being recorded in different languages, and in salvation being proclaimed to all ethnic groups" (Sunquist 2013:180).

Wright points out that, in fact, "in evangelistic contexts in the New Testament, there is unambiguous repudiation of the polytheistic worldview, but we do not find public denunciations of specific gods or offensive mockery of their worshiper" and that "prophetic voices address their denunciation of idolatry to the people of God themselves" (Wright 2006:185). In other words, the apostles, and Paul in particular, did not set out to be offensive in their call to turn people from false gods. This is true. In our final chapter we will argue that the example of Paul is, in fact, a better paradigm for the church's mission than that presented by *missio Dei.*

4

The Development of a "Missional Hermeneutic" Based on *Missio Dei*

♦ ♦ ♦

THE BASIC tenets described in the previous chapters are derived from a missional hermeneutic which, as has already been pointed out, developed after the tenets themselves had been embraced.

Before the development of missional hermeneutics the question arose as to whether there even is such a thing as a biblical basis for missions if it morphs over time. Bosch's description of mission paradigms in the course of church history can easily lead to the conclusion that the church is "a phenomenon of world history which can be grasped in historical and psychological and sociological terms like any other" (Bosch 1980:232).

However, the idea that there is no biblical paradigm for mission was difficult for evangelicals to swallow. Bosch himself didn't. Merely seeking a biblical foundation for the model was, however, also deemed insufficient, something dismissed as mere proof-texting, turning the Bible into "a mine from which we extract our gems—'missionary texts'" which may "not even provide an adequate whole-Bible grounding for mission" (Wright 2006:36). Sunquist concurs:

> Many missiological works begin with the Scripture, as if what is recorded in the Bible can be directly applied to a local church or mission agency today. The tendency is to pull out favorite verses to support a particular view, neglecting the more inclusive biblical meaning of mission. Most 'Bible-basis' mission approaches utilize direct commands and specific 'going' texts. Mission, however, is much bigger and more pervasive than a few important texts; the entire Bible is a missiological text (Sunquist 2013:174).

The aversion for "proof-texting" is understandable. After all, if the church's agenda is to be defined by the missionary nature of the Triune God then, logically, the Bible should be interpreted accordingly as well. And to do that you need a "missional hermeneutic" by which all of scripture is interpreted in the light of God's mission. Recognizing this, David Bosch floated the idea of creating a missional hermeneutic in an article he wrote in 1993 for the *Evangelical Review of Theology*.

Since then a number of different mission-based hermeneutics have evolved. A year after Bosch's article James Brownson of Western Theological Seminary wrote an article entitled "Speaking the Truth in Love: Elements of a Missional Hermeneutic", in which he proposed a "hermeneutic of diversity". Plural interpretations as a result of cultural diversity should be taken as a sign of interpretative effectiveness if it results in the gospel being perceived as an expression of the universal, salvific purpose of God.

> Diverse meanings of the Bible find a point of coherence, not in some 'standard' or universally accepted way of reading the Bible, but in the awareness that the God whose presence calls forth a distinctive form of doxology in their culture is the same God whose mercy calls forth grateful praise as well from other cultures, in other forms (Brownson 1994:486).

Many theologically conservative evangelicals would have difficulty accepting the premise of a multiplicity of valid meanings.

The missional hermeneutic with which Darrel Guder of Princeton Theological Seminary is associated is derived from his conviction that the purpose of the New Testament is to equip churches for witness. That being the case the fundamental question with which we should approach the text is "How did this text equip and shape God's people for their missional witness then, and how does it shape us today?" or, put another way, "How did this particular text continue the formation of witnessing communities then, and how does it do that today" (Guder, quoted in Hunsberger 2011:313). Critics might suggest that there are other reasons besides witness which moved the authors of the New Testament, such as worship, assurance of salvation, etc.

Michael Barram's idea of a missional hermeneutic consists of having the entire community ask a range of focused, critical and located questions regarding the church's purpose in order to discern the faith community's calling and task within the *missio Dei* (Hunsberger 2011:314). These "inherently contextual" questions should also be "precisely the kinds of important missional questions my social conditioning has conditioned me to overlook" (Baram, quoted in Hunsberger :316). It is not easy to see how what he is proposing differs substantially from a good Bible study in which the group asks challenging questions of the text and seeks to apply it to its own situation, since the model does not necessarily exclude proper exegesis.

The person within the evangelical world who worked out a missional hermeneutic in greatest detail is Christopher Wright. He contends that we need to move "beyond a biblical foundation for mission" (Wright 2006:34) (in other words, beyond simply tying Christian missions to a number of classic missionary passages) and, instead, evaluate missionary praxis on the basis of "a missiological framework of biblical theology" (:38). Essentially this means that the framework through which the entire Biblical narrative should be interpreted is the story of God's mission to the world, and that the covenant communities (Israel and, later, the church) which he has called into being, join Him in His divine, global task.

What, then, are the main contours of this missional hermeneutic which has taken the evangelical world by storm? We draw mainly, though not exclusively, from Wright's book *The Mission of God* (2006).

4.1. The Bible is both the story of God's mission and the product of God's mission

Mission is seen as the Bible's "grand narrative" (part of the subtitle of *The Mission of God*). According to Wright "the whole Bible renders to us the story of God's mission through God's people in their engagement with God's world for the sake of the whole of God's creation" (Wright 2006:51).

> The Old Testament tells its story as *the* story or, rather, as part of that ultimate and universal story that will ultimately embrace the whole of creation, time, and humanity within its scope. In other words, in reading these texts we are invited to embrace a metanarrative, a grand narrative (italics in original, 2006:55).

We are called to "read the Bible in the light of this great, overarching perspective of the mission of God" (:64).

4.2. The Bible should be interpreted in the light of God's love, grace and compassion

As already seen, love is perceived as the fundamental, driving attribute of God. That being the case everything else that we know about him must be seen through that prism. God's love, grace and compassion are the key concepts to understanding his revelation of himself. Thus God's compassionate nature causes his grace to trump his law. Echoing Bosch, Wright speaks of "the fundamental priority of grace over law" (Wright 2006:59), while Sunquist states that "the whole message of the Bible is the story of God's love for and relationship with his creation" (Sunquist 2013:181). He calls the Bible a "love story":

> The Bible is a love story, the story of a loving God who will not let go and watch his people reap their own destruction. He is constantly sending (mission), reminding, calling, forgiving, and judging. His concern is for all of creation, because, unlike the gods of the nations, he is the creator of all peoples and places. All of the inhabited earth and every nation is his (2013:183).

In short, "one of the key words for understanding the New Testament's essentially missionary character, is the word *compassion*" (italics in original, Bosch 1993:447), and everything we know about God must be interpreted in that light.

4.3. God's mission flows from the "creation mandate" and the fact that man is created in God's image

According to Sunquist "the first word in a mission theology is not 'savior' or 'salvation' but 'creator' and 'creation'" (Sunquist 2013:184), while Bosch maintains that "in creation God was already the God of mission, with his Word and Spirit as 'Missionaries'" (Bosch 1980:239). This is so because the creation story is presented as one of blessing: "Blessing then, in this foundational creation account, is constituted by fruitfulness, abundance and fullness on the one hand, and by enjoying rest within creation in holy and harmonious relationship with the Creator on the other" (Wright 2006:208). These blessings are meant for one and all: "The blessings of creation continue and are showered on all" (:214).

According to Wright the fact that "creation is intrinsically good" gives the earth "intrinsic value, that is to say, it is valued by God, who is the source of all value. God values the earth because he made it and owns it… Accordingly we need to be careful to locate an ecological dimension of mission not primarily in the need-supplying value of the earth to us, but in the glory-giving value of the earth to God" (Wright 2006:399).

The fact that humanity was given the task of filling, subduing and ruling over the earth forms one basis for a wholistic approach to missions: "Out of this understanding of our humanity… flows our ecological responsibility, our economic activity involving work, productivity, exchange and trade, and the whole cultural mandate" (2006:65).

> The physical and ecological character of the biblical visions of redemption offers the hope that the restoration of ecological harmony does lie within the possibilities of a redeemed human history: this… rather affirms that human societies will seek to revere God and to mirror his justice, will also produce the fruits of justice and equity in human moral order and harmony in the natural world (Wright 2006:410).

Wright describes in some detail the urgent ecological issues facing the planet, suggesting that this presents a "prophetic opportunity for the church" (:417).

Much is also derived from the truth that at creation God created man "in his image" (Gen. 1:27). First of all, this means this God can communicate with anyone:

> The living Creator God of all flesh needs no permission, no translation, no cross-cultural contextualization when he chooses to communicate with any person whom he has made in his own image. To be human is to be addressable by one's Creator… Even rebels and sinners are people made in God's image who are capable of hearing God's voice (Wright 2006:422).

The fact that people are created in God's image also leads to the conclusion that mankind shares a common ethic to which they will be held accountable: "There are common ethical bridges to people of all cultures. There is some universal sense of moral obligation that human beings share, which again is an important missiological foundation" (2006:423).

Furthermore, the fact that people are created in God's image gives everyone dignity and equality, and a claim on our love:

> When we look at any other person, we do not see the label (Hindu, Buddhist, Muslim, secular atheist, white, black, etc) but the image of God. We see someone created by God, addressed by God, accountable to God, loved by God, valued and evaluated by God… The validity of evangelism in principle does not legitimize any and every method of evangelism in practice… Anything that denies other human beings their dignity or fails to show respect, interest and informed understanding for all they hold precious is actually a failure of love (2006:423-424).

Individual human beings derive their meaning not only from the fact that they are created in God's image, but also because they are part of God's "good creation". Wright makes this point very forcefully:

> So the earth has intrinsic value—that is to say, it is valued by God, who is the source of all value. God values the earth because he made it and owns it. It is not enough merely to say that the earth is valuable to us. On the contrary, our own value as human beings begins from the fact that we ourselves are part of the whole creation that God already values and declares to be good… the starting point is that we take our value from the creation of which we are a part, not vice versa (Wright 2006:399).

4.4. Particular Biblical acts and events are seen as paradigmatic

God realized his universal mission through particular acts and events which became paradigmatic. The first example is God's call of and promise to Abraham to make his descendants, the people of Israel, a blessing to the wider world. "Ultimately all peoples of all nations will find blessing through Abraham… God has indeed made such blessing for all nations available through the Messiah, Jesus of Nazareth, the seed of Abraham" (Wright 2006:221). Thus God's mission to the nations can be summed up as follows: God elected

Israel to become a means of blessing to the nations because God wants them to know him, in spite of the fact that they are under his judgement. In the Abrahamic covenant God is perceived as using a particular means to further his universal purpose of blessing: "This universality of God's purpose, that nevertheless embraces the particularity of God's chosen means, is a recurrent theme" (:65).

The exodus also "stands as a paradigmatic and highly repeatable model for the way God wishes to act in the world, and ultimately will act for the whole of creation. The exodus is a prime lens through which we see the biblical mission." This means that "our commitment to mission must demonstrate the same broad totality of concern for human need that God demonstrated in what he did for Israel" (2006:275).

> The exodus narrative, then, makes it clear that two things in combination motivated divine action in redemption: the sight and sound of human misery under oppression, and the thought of God's own promise and purpose… On the one hand he is pulled down by human cries to investigate and rectify injustice on earth. On the other hand he is driven forward by his own declared intention to bless the nations and fulfill his covenant to Abraham (2006:273-274).

"The exodus, then, was indeed deliverance from slavery to sin—not Israel's own sin, but *the sin of those who oppressed them*" (italics in original, :278). This is quite a different interpretation of the older, classical take on the exodus which did not see it as a kind of paradigm of social redemption or a pattern for the church's mission to the world, but as a type or illustration of what spiritual redemption involved: the salvation of something much greater than political redemption — salvation from sin (Mat. 2:15; Eph. 1:7, Col. 1:13-14).

Another Old Testament event presented as a missiological paradigm is Israel's Year of Jubilee, which models "the wholeness of the church's evangelistic mission, its personal and social ethics and its future hope" (Wright 2006:300). As such, it is "about restoring to people the capacity to participate in the economic life of the community for their own viability and society's benefit… practical concern for the family unit… to restore social dignity and participation of families through maintaining or restoring their economic viability…. Jubilee speaks volumes to the massive issue of international debt…" (:297-298).

4.5. Jesus Christ plays multiple roles in the realization of God's mission

We have already seen how the emphasis on the person of Jesus Christ sets the evangelical version of *missio Dei* apart from the older, liberal version. In this section we look at how different aspects of his person and ministry are perceived as being of hermeneutical importance; in other words, how we are called to interpret our Bibles in light of the following aspects of his life and ministry.

4.5.1. Because Jesus Christ and YHWH share the same identity, their missions are one and the same

Because Jesus shares the identity of YHWH of the Old Testament, there is no difference of purpose between the Old Testament's presentation of YHWH as "the God who wills to be known" and the purpose of Jesus Christ (Wright 2006:106).

> Jesus then, according to the consistent witness of many strands in the New Testament documents, shares the identity of YHWH, the Lord God of Israel, and performs functions that were uniquely and exclusively the prerogative of YHWH in the Old Testament. These include God's role as Creator and owner of the universe, Ruler of history, Judge of all nations and Saviour of all who turn to him. In all of these dimensions of God's identity and activity, New Testament believers saw the face of Jesus, spoke of him in exactly the same terms and worshipped him accordingly (2006:122).

Biblical monotheism thus comes to mean that the persons of Jesus and God are one to such an extent that their purposes for being are one and the same: "Jesus then is associated with all that the Old Testament Scriptures affirm about God as Creator. Since creation forms the platform of God's mission in history... the centrality of Christ in that great mission of God within and for creation is clearly focused" (2006:113).

4.5.2. *Jesus Christ embodied and modeled Israel's wholistic mission of love and grace to the world*

Jesus Christ, as Israel's Messiah, is seen as embodying and fulfilling Israel's mission (Wright 2006:519), something he is perceived as spelling out in the "Nazareth Manifesto" of Luke 4:18-30, where he proclaims his "clearest programmatic statement". Jesus, in quoting directly from Isaiah 61, communicated that "his radical mission was the very mission of God found in the Old Testament proclamation of Jubilee" (:301).

Sunquist puts Jesus' "Nazareth Manifesto" at the very core of his message and life inasmuch as it proclaims how he would realize Israel's vision of God's kingdom. We quote at length:

> If anything is clear in Jesus, it is that the announcement and demonstration of the Kingdom are at the very core of his message and life.... The good news of the Kingdom includes the restoring of right relationships in the prophecies in the Old Testament—a new social order marked by *shalom*—and this included liberation from illnesses, diseases, and demons. To be blind or lame was to be poor, so healing meant restoration to society, the ability to work and contribute to family and community. Children were marginalized—the Kingdom of Jesus Christ brought children to the center of God's realm (Matt. 18:1-10). Women were considered inferior to men—Jesus healed them, touched them, and restored them to the community (Matt. 8:1-4, etc). And, of course, if demons have been cast out, 'then the kingdom of God has come upon you' (Matt 12:28). The Kingdom of God is judgment on other lords and kings, it is liberation, and it is the subsequent restoration of God's righteous rule. It is announced and demonstrated, and it is entered through the doorway of repentance. Missionaries, sent as Jesus was sent, proclaim the Kingdom of God in their presence and praxis (Sunquist 2013:220).

In short, Jesus' words and deeds of grace are seen as trumping vengeance and condemnation. Bosch concurs by pointing out that on three occasions where Jesus quotes the Torah, including the "Nazareth Manifesto", (Mat. 11:5-6; Luke 4:18-20; 7:22-23) he "deliberately stops short of the announcement about vengeance! How unimaginable! To read only the portion about grace, not the portion about vengeance! This was unforgiveable, especially as it implied that the same attitude would be expected of his followers" (Bosch 1993:448).

4.5.3. The cross of Christ is God's wholistic answer to the problems of sin plaguing the world

The evangelicals recognize that forgiveness of sin is available in the cross. Wright affirms that "only in the cross is there forgiveness, justification and cleansing for guilty sinners. Only in the cross stands the defeat of evil powers. Only in the cross is there release from the fear of death and its ultimate destruction altogether. Only in the cross are even the most intractable of enemies reconciled" (Wright 2006:315). He eloquently underlines the importance of the cross in overcoming evil and liberating humanity:

> God's mission was that: Sin should be punished and sinners forgiven; Evil should be defeated and humanity liberated; Death should be destroyed and human life and immortality brought to light; Enemies should be reconciled to one another and to God; Creation itself should be restored and reconciled to its Creator. All of these constitute the mission of God, and all of these led to the cross of Christ (Wright 2006:313-314).

4.6. Sin is idolatry, brokenness and oppression

Because people worship idols, the world is a broken place in which people are oppressed, God's image in them distorted, and God deprived of the glory due him: "A missiological perspective of idolatry, then, must include some analysis of the roots of the gods we made for ourselves" (Wright 2006:171) so that we can expose them for what they are: idols which deprive God of his glory, distort God's image in us, and lead to disappointment.

> The idols, gods, demons, and spiritual powers against which we declare war in the name of the gospel of Christ and his cross are things that oppress and ravage human existence. False gods destroy and devour lives, health and resources; they distort and diminish our humanity; they preside over injustice, greed, perversion, cruelty, lust and violence… Spiritual warfare is a matter of deep compassion for those oppressed by the forces of evil and idolatry—with all their

> attendant social, economic, political, spiritual and personal effects. We battle idolatry because, like the God whose mission we thereby share, we know that in doing so we seek the best interests of those we are called to serve in his name. We combat idolatry not only to glorify God but also to bless humanity. Spiritual warfare, like all forms of biblical mission, is to be motivated by and exercised with profound love, humility and compassion—as modeled in Jesus himself (Wright 2006:179).

Thus the church's mission is "to work with God in exposing the idols that continue to blur the distinction [of God as creator and of creation as that which is for our use and blessing], and to liberate men and women from the destructive delusions they foster" (2006:165). Wright later devotes multiple pages to describe sin's effects on human society and history, all of which "led to doubt the truth and goodness of God, thus undermining the prior relationship of trust and obedience" as a result of which "we are alienated from God, fearful of his presence, suspicious of his truth, hostile to his love" (:430).

In short, the missiological implication of wide-ranging idolatry and brokenness is for us to join God in his battle against such brokenness, alienation and idolatry:

> Since God's mission is to restore creation to its full original purpose of bringing all glory to God himself and thereby enable all creation to enjoy the fullness of blessing that he desires for it, God battles against all forms of idolatry and calls us to join him in that conflict (2006:188).

4.7. God's mission reflects His loving care for the nations

Wright sums up the Old Testament vision of the nations as follows:

> All nations of the world were created by YHWH, stand under his government in their historical affairs, are accountable to him morally and especially for the doing of justice. Like Israel, however, all nations have fallen short of the glory of God and stand in the same default position: under God's judgement... But beyond judgement there is hope, for there is always hope with the God of Israel...

> Ultimately the remnant of the nations will turn to the only saving God, YHWH (Wright 2006:500).

The New Testament, for its part, brings "the whole Old Testament story of Israel to its climax and destination, as the purpose for which God created Israel in the first place—the blessing of all nations—now becomes a reality through the mission of the church" (2006:514). Thus the New Testament "picks up and brings to fruition all the theology and expectation of the Old Testament in relation to God and the nations" (:505).

4.8. The purpose of election is to be a blessing to the world

God's people are elected, chosen, in order that they become a blessing to the rest of mankind, indeed to all of creation: "There was a universal purpose in God's election of Abraham, and therefore also a universal dimension to the very existence of Israel. Israel as a people was called into existence because of God's mission to bless the nations and restore his creation" (Wright 2006:251).

"The election of Israel is fundamentally missional, not just soteriological" (2006:263). In other words, election must be seen as instrumental, set in the context of God's universal plan for the nations, whose plan of salvation was set in motion by election. Thus divine election is more proof of God's deep love for the world: "We might paraphrase John 3:16 in a way that John would doubtless accept: 'God so loved *the world* that he chose Abraham and called Israel'" (italics in original, :263).

5

Missio Dei's Portrayal of a Salvation-Oriented Theology of Mission

♦ ♦ ♦

BEFORE PRESENTING our critiques of certain aspects of *missio Dei* we list some of the ways it critiques the older, salvation-oriented missionary enterprise. The almost irrepressible urge to belittle, mock, and parody the older model of theological understanding by some major proponents of a movement which is keen to work with virtually everyone else is very sad.[3] It is hard to escape the impression that many of its proponents are embarrassed by—and thus keen to disassociate themselves from—the salvation-of-the-soul, Christian discipleship, church-planting model of their theological fathers. Instead of rising to the defence of those who both modeled and proclaimed the gospel of God's saving grace in Jesus Christ when virtually no one else was, they have largely bought into the stereotypes of their own heritage.

5.1. Proponents of previous missiological models are "less spiritual"

Firstly, there are those advocates of *missio Dei* who suggest that those who hold to the older view of missions are less spiritual: "There is a need for some evangelicals to… rediscover a theocentric view of mission which emphasizes character and spirituality over activity. *Missio Dei* and reflection on what many see as the key verse for

[3] NOTE: In personal correspondence with me Christopher Wright stated unequivocally that he disassociates himself from those who belittle, mock or parody the older missionary models or practices, and pointed out that his own parents went out with WEC to the Amazon back in the 1920s, that they led many to Christ and established churches which continue to exist today.

trinitarian misson, John 20:21, could provide the missing dimension." (Arthur 6/2013).

David Bosch maintains that "evangelicals emphasize that everything in this world is temporary, relative, and therefore unimportant" and that they uncritically uphold the established order. He then equates them with religious Nazis who "could, for instance, be the ideal family man and piously go to Church on Sunday, but for the rest participate, without any pangs of conscience, in the extermination of the Jews" (Bosch 1980:207). This is not merely offensive, it is also grossly inaccurate, if only by virtue of the broad, sweeping nature of the allegation. He then extrapolates a non-sequitur which suggests that "this kind of selective conservatism also reveals itself where evangelicals, on the one hand, lament the increasing secularisation of all areas of life and, on the other hand, accept all the technical products and achievement of secularisation as proofs of 'divine providence' (Bosch:208).

Bosch also perceived evangelicals as incapable of enjoying the good things of creation:

> Evangelicals tend to regard the world in which we live as essentially evil, surrendered to the 'prince of this world' (John 16:11; cf. 1 John 5:19). The Christian may not enjoy this world; rather he should consistently shun 'the things of this world'. After all, his citizenship is in heaven. Contact with the world should therefore be reduced to the minimum (Bosch 1980:32).

In fact, the evangelicals' view of creation smacks of Gnosticism: "Gnosticism has a pessimistic view of the material world, and a salvation that is partial (only the spiritual is redeemed)" (Sunquist 2013:185). Their version of the gospel is a type of easy believism: "the gospel is here sometimes understood as primarily a 'subject for belief' rather than 'a way of life'. It is a message which, if 'accepted', guarantees entrance into the Kingdom" (Bosch 1980:31).

> It should come as no surprise that often the planting of churches on the mission field received scant attention. The essential thing is that people are 'won for Christ'; their incorporation into an ecclesiastical organization is of secondary importance. The Church as institution and organization may even be considered a handicap to the spiritual growth of converts (1980:34).

On what basis these conclusions are drawn and how widespread this mentality is, is not addressed.

5.2. The older model is culturally inappropriate in a pluralistic world

As Eddie Arthur puts it in an article for World magazine, "the traditional declamatory — confrontational, even — evangelical approach to mission is becoming increasingly less culturally appropriate as pluralism expands" (Arthur 06/2013). Because the previous generation's missionary movement "largely coincided with the West's colonizing of the non-Western world, it was inevitably mixed with overtones of Western superiority, imperialism, power and know-how and with the idea of the 'haves' and the 'have-nots' (Bosch 1993:440). Thus "the evangelical tendency to withdraw from the world for fear of defilement is, strangely enough, often coupled with the idea of viewing the world as a territory that has to be invaded and its prisoners liberated. In this way parts of the world can be reclaimed for God" (Bosch 1980:35).

In other words, the idea of liberating people, such a major theme of *missio Dei*, is considered culturally inappropriate when thought of in spiritual terms.

5.3. The older model is portrayed as theologically and hermeneutically simplistic

The older approach is dismissed because it is based on "inadequate proof-texting"—no matter how many biblical texts there are to reference:

> whether one text or many, the danger that attends all proof-texting is still present. We have already decided what we want to prove (that our missionary practice is biblical), and our collection of texts simply ratifies our perception. The Bible is turned into a mine from which we extract our gems—'missionary texts'. These texts may indeed sparkle, but simply laying out such gems on a string is not yet what one could call a missiological hermeneutic of the whole Bible itself. It does not even provide adequate whole-Bible grounding for mission (Wright 2006:36).

Wright's statement is taken almost verbatim from an article written by Bosch: "the Bible was used as a mine from which 'missionary texts' could be extracted… if we searched carefully and persistently among the rocks and rubble we would find small nuggets of real gold—stores of pagans such as Ruth and Naaman" (Bosch 1993:439).

Proof-texting is presented as bad because those who do so are seen as "obviously" foisting their own preconceived notions about the nature of Christian missions on the reader:

> When theologians with preconceived ideas about mission… look at the Bible, it is obvious that they would judge that at least the Old Testament reveals a 'thoroughly passive character' as far as mission is concerned. The same verdict has often been made about the Jesus of the gospels: the idea of a mission to the pagan world lay entirely outside his horizon (Bosch 1993:440).

Wright holds that the older model is based on a "military style command" (i.e. the Great Commission) which has

> so tightly bound our understanding of mission to a single (and undeniably crucial) imperative of Jesus that we have difficulty making connections between mission and the rest of the Scriptures, where those other Scriptures are not obviously or grammatically imperative. We do not perceive any missional authority in such non-imperative texts because we conceive authority only in terms of commands (Wright 2006:52).

It is understandable why the attack on this point is worded as strongly as it is: *missio Dei* can only displace the older model in the evangelical mind if it can lay claim to some kind of higher biblical ground than the actual commands and instructions of Jesus Christ and the model of the apostle Paul.

5.4. The long history of generations of faithful missionary social service is belittled

David Bosch is particularly acerbic in his attacks on the older evangelical model's history of faithful social service. As far as he was concerned, the dastardly motivation behind such services was the desire for "the verbal proclamation of an other-worldly message and a preparation for the hereafter. Consequences of mission, such as social and political changes, were, in essence, regarded as by-products. Other activities of missionary societies, such as education and medical care, were only ancillaries to the verbal proclamation of the gospel" (Bosch 1993:440). Elsewhere he wrote disparagingly that:

> Schools, hospitals, orphanages and the like are primarily seen as instruments affording pupils, patients and orphans the opportunity of hearing the gospel. By attending to man's body (for instance in the hospital) or mind (in the mission school), they are preparing him for the gospel. The success of mission schools and hospitals is often judged according to the number of converts they produce (Bosch 1980:33).

In their supposed "reticence in the area of addressing themselves directly to the wrongs in the structures of society—racial discrimination, migratory labour, economic and political exploitation, etc.—evangelicals are often seen as siding with the existing political order. In the expression 'conservative evangelical' the word 'conservative' frequently seems to cover both the theological and political aspects" (1980:34).

Wright asks:

> How then can it be suggested that evangelistic proclamation is the only essential mission of the church? It seems impossible to me to justify such reductionism if we intend to sustain any claim to be taking the whole Bible seriously as our authority for mission and as that which defines the content and scope of our mission (2006:306).

He warns of the danger of an exclusively spiritualized form of mission into which, according to him, particular generations of missionaries seem to have fallen as a result of ignoring the range of narrative and poetic texts. He concludes that this

> means that the gospel is presented only as a means of having your own sins forgiven and having assurance of a future with God in heaven—without either the moral challenge of walking with personal integrity in the world of social, economic and political society around us, or the missional challenge of being actively concerned for issues of justice and compassion for others. The result is a kind of privatized pietism" which can "even make a virtue out of paying little attention to the physical, material, familial, societal and

> international needs and crises that abound on every side (2006:287).

Several chapters further, however, he thankfully points out that:

> In the past Christians have instinctively been concerned about the great and urgent issues in every generation, and rightly included them in their overall concept of mission calling and practice. These have included the evils of disease, ignorance, slavery, and many other forms of brutality and exploitation. Christians have taken up the cause of widows, orphans, refugees, prisoners, the insane, the hungry... (2006:413).

The point we seek to make here is that history is rife with examples for just about anything one wants to prove. The kind of cherry-picking which Bosch, in particular, engages in to build his case against previous generations of evangelical missionaries is unworthy of an otherwise great scholar.

6

Critical Concerns about *Missio Dei*

♦ ♦ ♦

PROPONENTS OF *missio Dei* will undoubtedly take exception to many of the following critiques and point to refutations made by its major defenders. And, in all fairness, some of its leading evangelical proponents do not, in fact, embrace some of the positions outlined below. In a model of missions which is as diverse as *missio Dei*, which embraces as much as it does, and which has morphed considerably over time, both critics and defenders can finds statements about anything they want to affirm. Logically and theologically speaking, however, the following critiques highlight problems with respect to some of the model's fundamental propositions.

6.1. *Missio Dei* de-emphasizes the idea of sinful man in his natural state as an object of God's wrath, particularly in evangelistic contexts

The Bible's view of the natural man as an object of God's wrath (see, for instance, Mark 7:21-22; Luke 13:1-5; John 8:24; Rom. 1:18-2:5; 5:12-19; Eph. 2:13) is muted, particularly in evangelistic contexts. Wright points out that divine wrath was something Paul talked about when addressing Christians. In his speeches to pagans he "highlights God's kindness, providence and patience" (Wright 2006:182).

Bosch, for his part, is both accurate and disparaging when describing the older evangelical missionary's motive as having to do with sin:

> Man's greatest anguish is his lostness before God, his greatest need to be saved from his sins and reconciled to God, his greatest fear for eternal punishment in hell, his greatest hope for eternal glory in the hereafter. Sin, in this

> definition, has to do primarily with man's relationship to God which has gone wrong. It is, moreover, something personal and individual (Bosch 1980:-31-32).

Bosch is not alone among proponents of *missio Dei* popular among evangelicals today who do not view sin as an offense to a holy God resulting in a world languishing under divine judgement, whether in time or eternity (hell).

> 'To save' is a transitive verb. One must be saved from something and to something. Jesus saves… from exile and slavery. Whether people realize it, acknowledge it, or avoid it, sin is the ever-present enemy of every human being, dragging us down to sickness, death and separation from God (Sunquist 2013:337).

Thus sin as personal, individual, and pertaining primarily to man's culpability before God, and not just separation from Him, is either rejected or glossed over. The idea that "against you [God], you only have I sinned and done what is evil in you sight, so you are right in your verdict and justified when you judge" (Psalm 51:4) is either de-emphasized or disregarded altogether. Instead, it is presented as brokenness, or as a type of exile, or as enslavement to something which controls us and from which we need to be liberated. In other words, sin is bad because of its bad effects on people. It is not defined in terms of how it affects man's relationship with God, but in the way it affects people. It is defined by what we are saved from, not by whom we have offended.

Little wonder that the concept of Christ's crucifixion as satisfying God's wrath is virtually excised by many proponents of *missio Dei*, even though that was the "sound doctrine" Paul urged Timothy to "preach in season and out of season" (2 Tim. 2:4-5).[4] One could argue, in fact, that particularly among proponents who hold more

---

[4] NOTE: Christopher Wright strongly affirms substitutionary atonement. For instance, in his book *The God I Don't Understand* (Zondervan, 2008) he states that "It (i.e. the cross) involved Christ identifying himself with our sin in his death in such a way that God no longer counts our sin against us and thus enables reconciliation to take place" (p. 120). Also, "substitution is not a metaphor for what God did' it is what he actually did. God actually did put himself in a place where we should be, to do for us what we could not do for ourselves" (p. 125).

liberal views, *missio Dei* has formed another front against the doctrine of penal substitutionary atonement, which is already under siege.[5]

The great question which drives the biblical narrative — particularly from the perspective of Paul's epistles — is "How can lost, sinful, rebellious people who by nature are 'objects of God's wrath' (Rom. 9:22-23; Eph. 2:3), be reconciled to and live in the presence of that perfectly holy, righteous God?" There is only one answer to that question, and it runs through the entirety of the Bible's progressive revelation: by means of the sacrifice God himself would provide. This gospel seems too reductionist for many who embrace *missio Dei.* Thankfully, there are theologically conservative apologists of the model, like Wright, who continue to affirm these truths. *Missio Dei* is an aviary containing birds of very different theological plumage!

6.2. *Missio Dei* denies that God's love is mediated solely through the cross

As we have repeatedly seen, the proponents of *missio Dei* celebrate the love of God as his attribute *par excellence.* C.S. Song, former president of the World Alliance of Reform Churches, approvingly spells out the logical consequences:

> Theology of compassion is the theology of love with no strings attached to it… it does not assume that God left Asia in the hands of pagan powers and did not come to it until missionaries of the West reached it. That would have left Asia without the God of Jesus for millions of years. Jesus' God could not have been such an irresponsible God (Song 1985:167).

The problem with this is that *missio Dei* makes no distinction between God's governing work and his saving work, as a result of which God's love is seen as operating outside the cross as well as through it. This is logically quite possible if one glosses over man's legal culpability before a holy God. However, there is hardly a verse in the New Testament which speaks of God's love that does not also speak of the cross (see, for example, John 3:16, Gal. 2:20; Rom. 5:8; 1 John

---

[5] See, for instance, McGowan, ATB. Ed. 2006. "The Atonement as Penal Substitution", Pages 183-210 in *Always Reforming: Explorations in Systematic Theology*. Downers Grove: Intervarsity Press.

4:10). The reason is clear: although everyone may enjoy God's common grace and governing work (i.e. his non-salvific graces which keep the world from becoming a hell), the all-embracing foundation of God's love which proponents of *missio Dei* so celebrate is, in fact, mediated through the risen Christ alone, and thus only available to those whose sins have been atoned for on the cross. To speak of the blessings of the gospel of God's grace in Jesus Christ without preaching the gospel of the cross is, to use DeYoung and Gilbert's striking illustration, like

> picking up an armful of leaves and insisting you're holding a tree. Unless those leaves are connected to the trunk, you don't have a tree; you just have an armful of dead leaves. In the same way, unless the blessings of the gospel of the kingdom are connected to the cross, you don't have a gospel at all (DeYoung & Gilbert 2011:108).

The gospel is not simply declaring that the kingdom of God has come but also declaring that one can enter it through repentance of sin, faith in Christ's substitutionary atonement and resurrection from the dead, and the gift of the "new birth". Because certain major proponents of *missio Dei* seem to struggle with these key aspects of the apostle Paul's theology, let us instead quote the apostle Peter to make the same points:

> Repent, then, and turn to God, so that your sins may be wiped out, that times of refreshing may come from the Lord (Acts 3:19).

> Salvation is found in no one else [but Christ], for there is no other name under heaven given to mankind by which we must be saved (Acts 4:12).

> For Christ also suffered once for sins, the righteous for the unrighteous, to bring you to God (1 Peter 3:18).

> Praise be to the God and Father of our Lord Jesus Christ! In his great mercy he has given us new birth into a living hope through the resurrection of Jesus Christ from the dead (1 Peter 1:3).

> He commanded us to preach to the people and to testify that he [Christ] is the one whom God appointed as judge of the living and the dead (Acts 10:42).

The last verse leads us to the next point.

6.3. Major proponents of *missio Dei* downplay divine judgement and hell as motives for mission

The subject index of Michael Goheen's 440 page book *Introducing Christian Mission Today* makes no reference whatsoever to the subject of hell. For his part, Scott Sunquist holds that

> there are some questions and issues that we cannot know the answer to in this life. Therefore it is best to set these issues aside for later times of private intellectual speculation and move on to what we do know. 1. We cannot know the actual state, condition, or place of hell. 2. We cannot know the actual state, condition or place of heaven. 3. We cannot know exactly who will be found in either place (although we may have some pretty good ideas). 4. We cannot know the fate of those who came before the death, resurrection and ascension of Jesus Christ, nor can we be sure of the fate of those who have never heard of Jesus Christ (Sunquist 2013:335).

These are remarkable affirmations of ignorance for someone in the business of training evangelical missionaries—after all, substantial biblically-based answers to these questions can be found in any of the many evangelical systematic theologies in print. By relegating talk about heaven and hell to the realm of "private intellectual speculation" you basically maintain that those subjects are as important as, say, how many angels can dance on the head of a pin. You are also cutting the nerve of Christian missions.

Instead of hell, Sunquist prefers to think in terms of "exile": "An understanding of the punishment of exile of those who are 'unfaithful' is a precondition for understanding Jesus' teachings" (Sunquist 2013:336). And he conceives of judgment not in terms of God holding people to account but of the conquest of evil power and the vanquishing of "idols":

> Grace is available because the evil powers have been vanquished. If there is no judgment of evil, there is no grace

> for others. The cross is a judgment on sin and death. The outworking of this gospel is seen in the rejection of all vanquished idols. Christian virtues are not possible and vices are hamstrung. Thus the gospel messages include the call to live into the new life, which recognizes the defeat of the other lords (2013:216).

David Bosch was also very uncomfortable with the idea of divine vengeance in time and in hell for eternity. He refers to the divine command to eliminate the Canaanites, whom God bore patiently for 400 years, as "incidental references to encounters between members of the biblical covenant people and the surrounding nations" (Bosch 1980:57) and makes no reference to Noah's Flood. He also points out that when Jesus spoke in the synagogue of his hometown Nazareth (the supposed "Nazareth Manifesto") he deliberately refrained from speaking about God's vengeance—but fails to note that Jesus often spoke about vengeance, hell, and the judgment to come elsewhere, more than anyone else in the scriptures.

In response we can do no better than to quote DeYoung and Gilbert, whose book *What is the Mission of the Church* I cannot recommend enough:

> Since hell is real, we must help each other die well even more than we strive to help our neighbors live comfortably. Since hell is real, we must never think alleviating earthly suffering is the most loving thing we can do. Since hell is real, evangelism and discipleship are not simply good options or commendable ministries, but are literally a matter of life and death. If we lose the doctrine of hell, either too embarrassed to mention it or too culturally sensitive to affirm it, we can count on this: the boat will drift. The cross will be stripped of propitiation, our preaching will be devoid of urgency and power, and our work in the world will no longer center on calling people to faith and repentance and building them to maturity in Christ (2011:245).

In the final analysis, obedience to the Great Commission must be the primary mission of the church to the world because at death each individual enters eternity into either heaven or hell. The eternal wellbeing of the human soul really, really matters—ultimately more than anything else. We close this section by, once again, quoting the apostle Peter:

> Though you have not seen him, you love him; and even though you do not see him now, you believe in him and are filled with an inexpressible and glorious joy, *for you are receiving the end result of your faith, the salvation of your souls* (1 Peter 1:8-9).

6.4. *Missio Dei* distorts Christ's mission

As seen earlier, *missio Dei* places great emphasis on Christ's incarnation and suffering as a model for missions. Within the evangelical world this "incarnational" model of missions was popularized by John Stott in his 1975 book *The Christian Mission in the Modern World: What the Church Should Be Doing Now*, followed up in 1992 with *The Contemporary Christian: Applying God's Word to Today's World.* Stott pushed this idea so far that, according to him, if a community deteriorates socially that is due to the failure of the church to function as salt and light (1975:32). Stott and all other protagonists of this model read much into John 20:21, where Jesus said, "As the Father has sent me, so send I you".

Köstenberger takes issue with the notion that John 20:21 means that missionaries are to adopt an incarnational model of missions.

> Not the way in which Jesus came into the world (i.e. incarnation), but the nature of Jesus' *relationship with his sender* (i.e. one of obedience and utter dependence), is presented in the Fourth Gospel as the model for the disciples' mission. Jesus' followers are called to imitate Jesus' selfless devotion in seeking his sender's glory, to submit to the sender's will, and to represent their sender accurately and know him intimately (Köstenberger 1998:217).

The German theologian Peter Beyerhaus (who has been ringing warning bells about *missio Dei* since the 1970s) notes the danger of a missiology which focuses on the humanity of Jesus and His service to the social needs of this world. "His divinity... is largely obliterated... In what could be called an 'example Christology' it is emphasized that the Incarnate Christ has made Himself a servant and led a life of service in the needs of mankind" (Beyerhaus 2013:5). He goes on to correct the idea that at a fundamental level Christ can be our model in missions:

> We need to understand that the matchless incarnation of the eternal Word of God (John 1:14), His once for all sacrificial death, and His ascension to the throne of God set up a

> barrier against any *imitatio Christi*. For his atoning sacrifice on the cross to take away our guilt cannot be imitated… Indeed, it is inadmissible to change the message of 'Christ for us' to the slogan 'Let us act like Christ', thereby making the gospel a new law (2013:5).

Missio Dei presents the person of Christ as the missionary's role model. But we are not Christ. He was God. He had the power to heal, to cast out demons, to raise the dead, to walk on water. Furthermore, wonderful as his miracles and ministry were to those touched by them, Jesus is clear that the purpose for these activities was to establish his identity as the one the prophets had spoken about, not primarily to meet the needs of the sick and the poor. "It is misleading to contend that Jesus' ministry focused on serving… Don't miss this fact: there is not a single example of Jesus going into a town with the stated purpose of healing or casting out demons" (DeYoung & Gilbert 2011:55, 56).

Jesus did not seek political office in order to advance his transformational agenda. He did not pursue political or social transformation in the current historical reality[6]—to the great disappointment of the crowds. Nor did the apostles, as they preached the gospel throughout the Roman Empire. Then why should we?

This doesn't mean that Jesus didn't care for the outcasts, the sick and the poor. Of course he did! But the purpose of his ministry was teaching people who he was, the nature of and standards for entry into the kingdom of God, the need for repentance and, toward the end of his ministry, what he was seeking to accomplish through his impending death and resurrection. "The mission of Jesus is not service broadly conceived, but the *proclamation* of the gospel through teaching, the *corroboration* of the gospel through signs and wonders, and the *accomplishment* of the gospel in death and resurrection" (italics in original, 2011:57). The purpose statements in the gospels make this clear: Jesus came to preach, to call sinners, and to give his life as a ransom for many (John 1:28; Mark 1:38, 2:17; 10:45).

As Christ's heralds the New Testament clearly commands us to follow in Christ's steps, particularly with respect to being willing to embrace suffering for his sake (1 Peter 2:21). As already seen, some *missio Dei* proponents make much of this fact: "*Missio Dei* is a matter

---

[6] Though if a sufficient number of socially very significant groups of people along with a sufficiently large number of others embrace Jesus' teachings that could very well happen.

of our participating with Jesus Christ in his suffering love for the greater glory of God to be revealed" (italics in original, Sunquist 2013:172).

> Christian mission is the church's participation in the Triune God through the suffering of Christ, who was sent by the Father for the redemption and liberation of the world, by means of the conversion of individuals and cultures, in the power of the Holy Spirit, to the end that God be glorified in the nations and in all of his creation (Sunquist 2013:173).

However, thinking of suffering as "participation in the Triune God" is reading rather a lot into the purposes of Christian suffering. It is, in fact, difficult to ascertain how much Sundquist wants us to read into his statement. In any case, important distinctions are once again blurred. While Christ's suffering saves, our suffering serves. His suffering propitiates and our suffering—at best—proclaims. His suffering serves as the heart of the gospel, our suffering is "granted by God" (Phil. 1:29) as a means of disciplining the individual Christian, as an agent to purify the church, to soften hearts, and to increase faith so that the believer will become more Christ-like in the process (1 Peter 1:6-7).

But does the Bible also present suffering as participation with God through Christ's suffering as a 'missionary method' which actually helps effect the redemption and liberation of the world by means of the conversion of individuals and cultures? I don't see it. It does not even present suffering as a gift of the Spirit given the church in order to minister effectively.

6.5. *Missio Dei* distorts the role of the church in missions

As we have seen, *missio Dei* places great emphasis on involvement in God's project of transforming and renewing all things. This means the church is "invited" to "participate" with God and with anyone else involved in any way in making the world a better place. This may include developing better medical services, teaching in national schools, digging wells, militating for ecologically responsible legislation, promoting better agricultural methods, sponsoring projects for orphans, and involvement in dozens of other such worthwhile projects which have little or no church connection.

As Beyerhaus points out, "by this view, He [God] could just as well use other instruments for this goal, such as non-Christian religions and political-social movements whose members might be atheists!" (Beyerhaus 2013:6). Should the Christian church really co-opt the world into its missionary enterprise?

> Non-Christians do not do 'kingdom work'. The phrase 'kingdom work' is confusing and non-biblical and should probably be jettisoned, but even if we grant its use we should at least be agreed that it cannot be applied to good things that non-Christians do. When a non-Christian does a good deed, it is most certainly good (at a certain level), and it is an instance of God's common evil-restraining grace on all mankind (DeYoung & Gilbert 2011:112).

For a theology of missions which questioned the role of the church in missions in the first place, as the earlier, more liberal versions of *missio Dei* did, working hand-in-glove with the world was not a problem. They "tended to radicalize the view that *missio Dei* was larger than the mission of the church, even to the point of suggesting that it *excluded* (italics in original) the churches' involvement" (Bosch 1991:401): "We have no business in 'articulating' God. In the final analysis, '*missio Dei*' means that God articulates himself, without any need of assisting him through our missionary efforts" (:402).

Fusing God's mission and the church's mission into one, by having the church shoulder the task of world transformation the contemporary evangelical version of *missio Dei* opened the way to one of the current phenomena of evangelical Christian mission: missionaries involved in various "churchless missionary activities". D. A. Carson is scathing on the matter:

> I know numerous groups that claim to be engaging in 'wholistic' ministry because they are helping the poor in Chicago or because they are digging wells in the Sahel, even though few, if any, of the workers have taken time to explain to anyone who Jesus is and what he has done to reconcile us to God. Their ministry isn't holistic; it's halfistic or quarteristic (Carson 2011).

Beyerhaus points out that when the church comes to be regarded in terms of her service to the world, its function becomes more important than its nature: "the church is seen and valued in another perspective. Here she is called to devote herself totally to service in the world, striving for economic, social and political change, so that in this way the kingdom of God might be made manifest step by step" (Beyerhaus 2013:6). DeYoung and Gilbert note that:

> One of the biggest missteps in much of the newer mission literature is an assumption that whatever God is doing in the world, this too is our task. So if the *missio Dei* (the mission of God) is ultimately to restore shalom and renew the cosmos, then we, as his partners, should work to the same ends... But what if we are not called to partner with God in all he undertakes? What if the work of salvation, restoration, and re-creation are divine gifts to which we bear witness, rather than works in which we collaborate? What if our mission is not identical with God's mission? What if we carry on Jesus' mission but not in the same way he carried it out? Isn't it better to locate our responsibility in the tasks we are given rather than in the work we see God accomplishing? In fact, there are certain things that God intends to do one day that we are to have no part in, and certainly not in this age. The slaying of the wicked comes to mind! (DeYoung & Gilbert 2011:42).

The church's primary missionary task is not serving the world, good and praiseworthy as that is. It is primarily called to be witnesses to God's grace in Christ, to be ambassadors of Christ who proclaim the good news of His atoning death and victorious resurrection which is available to all through repentance and faith (Acts 1:8; 5:42; 6:4,7; 22:15; 1 Cor. 9:16-23; Col. 1:28-29; 2 Tim. 4:1-2; 1 Peter 5:1), and the gathering of these "born again" ones into churches (Acts 14:21-23; 18:1-11). What good is a "wholistic ministry" if it doesn't, in the first place, focus on seeing people become "whole" again in Christ? Yet even otherwise strongly evangelical proponents of *missio Dei* are critical of the idea of placing a higher priority on evangelism than on social transformation:

> The language of 'priority' implies that all else is 'secondary' at best... In other words, the language of priority and primacy quickly tends to imply singularity and exclusion... We are back to so exalting the New Testament evangelistic mandate that we think it absolves us from all other dimensions of God's mission that the rest of the Bible requires of God's people... The word *priority* suggests something that has to be your starting point... However a different way of thinking

> about mission would be to imagine a whole circle of all the needs and opportunities that God calls (or sends) us to address in the world (italics in original, Wright 2006:317).

Wright goes on to speak of entering "the circle of missional response at any point on the circle of human need" and of not resting until our missional response reflects "the wholeness of God's missional response to the human predicament—and that of course included the good news of Christ, the cross and resurrection, the forgiveness of sin, the gift of eternal life that is offered to men and women through our witness to the gospel and the hope of God's new creation" (Wright 2006:319). The problem, of course, is that the proclamation of the gospel can easily become something which is tagged on to various types of "transformational activities", particularly when the church engages in these activities with people, governments and NGOs which do not share its basic world view.

In his second book on missions, *The mission of God's people: a biblical theology of the church's mission,* Wright makes no distinction between the specific task of the church and the way ordinary Christians should live out their Christian lives. It is excellent if read as a manual on how individual Christians should live their lives in the 21st century—the problem is spelled out in its title, which fuses everything Christians do with the church's mission. If evangelism is merely one of many aspects of mission, all of which are of equal importance, then the heart of missions has changed fundamentally. Indeed, if every good and positive thing falls under the rubric of *missio Dei* then the concept itself is emptied of specific meaning and, as a result, can be marshalled to support anything and everything. Like Hoedemaker a generation earlier, the missiologist Andrew Kirk, himself a proponent of *missio Dei*, complained that "*missio Dei* has been used to advance all kinds of missiological agendas" (Kirk 1999:45).

6.6. *Missio Dei*'s doctrinal imprecision leads to a host of problems

We have already seen how doctrines such has hell tend to be glossed over. Other classic doctrines are also given short shrift. For example, while *missio Dei*'s interpretation of election as God choosing a means through which he wants to bless the world is, of course, biblical (e.g. God chose Abraham as a means through which he would bless the world), the narrower teaching of divine election unto salvation does not easily fit the model. It is impossible to integrate either the Calvinist teaching that Christ died for a particular people, or the classic Arminian position that God's prevenient grace precedes regeneration, with *missio Dei*'s ideas about the huge, fountain-like love of God which embraces all people equally and seeks everyone's wellbeing without differentiation. (In fact the argument that love is God's defining attribute is not something every Christian would agree with. Many would argue that if God has a defining attribute it would be his holiness—hence holy love, holy anger, etc.). If the acceptance or rejection of God's indiscriminate love-overtures lies with mankind then the only theological underpinning which fits the model is semi-pelagianism.

The idea that the church is invited to participate with what God is doing in the world is also fraught with danger, for it undermines God's authority. God doesn't "invite" his people, he commands them. The Great Commission statements are the church's marching orders: "Go! Make disciples!" Much as major proponents of *missio Dei* play down those "military style commands", commands they are, given by the One who establishes the parameters and stipulations within which his people are to live and serve, and then sovereignly gives his people the necessary grace to carry out his commands.

By removing the church from its traditional position in missions as the enterprise's responsible agent, *missio Dei* risks eliminating the kind of accountability that mission agencies and missionaries might have felt towards the church in the past. Whether wittingly or not, proponents of *missio Dei* often tend to push towards a "self-regulating" (as in "we are responsible to God") missionary enterprise outside the control of the church which is, nevertheless, expected to finance the undertaking.

Another doctrinal distinction which *missio Dei* eliminates is the difference between God's salvific and common grace.

> We cannot state that God's activity with Israel is revelation while that with the other nations is mere providence. There is no such distinction between revelation and the rest of history, because God was involved with Israel, Assyria and Philistia all at once, in both their political and religious histories, and he will rule them all directly through his Messiah (Samuel & Sugden 1999:177).

This lack of distinction fudges the biblical idea that "all things work for the good of those who love him [God] and are called according to his purposes" (Rom. 8:28). Although God's common grace makes this world a liveable place for most of us, ultimately things only work out for good for those who meet the criteria of having been called by God and are living according to his purposes.

Yet another doctrinal problem with *missio Dei* is that it is all about what God is doing without asking questions about what Satan might be doing. The reality of two kingdoms, a kingdom of light and a kingdom of darkness, which are at war until Christ's second coming, is much more reflective of the actual teachings of the New Testament. Yes, God is the ruler of history, but His kingdom pertains to the spiritual realities which flow from Christ's redemptive work: the realignment of the wills of those who are regenerated by God's spirit and their formation into strongly counter-cultural communities, local churches whose value should be at odds with those of the world at large.

Nor does *missio Dei* allow for the possibility that God may choose to use evil both to discipline the body of believers and as an instrument leading to the eternal salvation of some. Habakkuk's and Asaph's questions (Psalm 73) about the purposes of evil and why the wicked are allowed to prosper while the righteous suffer are almost impossible to answer in a theology of all-encompassing divine love.

Of course such doctrinal imprecision allows for both wider ecumenical and intercultural engagement and cooperation, something which many of the model's protagonists celebrate:

> It must be remembered that many evangelicals pulled out of the WCC basically in protest that the ecumenical movement was reducing mission to social engagement. When they did so, there was very little conversation with either Roman Catholics or ecumenical Protestants. In the first decades of the twenty-first century we live in a different context. We now have a long history of evangelical and Roman Catholic dialogue on mission (1977-84), and evangelicals have a much greater engagement in issues of social justice as part of the work of evangelization. With these elements in place, there is the opportunity to develop greater trust and partnership across confessional boundaries (Sunquist 2013:165).

The problem here is the failure to recognize that Christian unity and ministry must be based on Christian love *and* truth. Sacrificing fundamental New Testament teachings is sacrificing one of the church's main missionary obligations: proclamation.

Doctrinal imprecision, the desire to re-engage ecumenically with non-evangelicals, the fact that the model has little use for the notion of hell, the idea that God's mission is not necessarily mediated through the church but that, at the same time, "the church must take with radical seriousness what is happening in the world… and take the world's agenda seriously" (Potter 1981:73-74), and a hyper-emphasis on the love of God divorced from the cross, whose compassion compelled him to act lovingly long before missionaries arrive on the scene, means that the current model of *missio Dei* has no firm anchor to keep it from slipping into the same universalism as its earlier predecessor.

> Does our refusal to segregate God's work among his own and other peoples into 'sacred' and 'secular' history mean that we deny any difference between special revelation and general revelation? God works in many different ways in different histories, but always with the same goal. If we used a distinction between special revelation and general revelation we would be assuming that God's special revelation is confined to his activities with either Israel or the church. Such an assumption is not biblical (Samuel & Sugden 1999:177).

From here it is but a small step to the position held by such liberal and pluralist scholars as W.C. Smith, who laud the missionary efforts of other religions:

> The mission of the church is not God's only mission. It is not even his only world-wide mission… Few of us Christians know much about God's mission in the Islamic venture, God's mission to India and nowadays to the world through the Hindu venture (Smith 1988:366).

None of the evangelicals considered in this book would go this far and some, like Wright, are strongly critical of such attitudes (see, for instance, his book *The Uniqueness of Jesus*). In my opinion, however, the trajectory of these teachings leads in this direction. Is God really present in other religions? Well, maybe there is some limited understanding of a creator God to whom people are accountable. God may be able to communicate with anyone, as Wright notes (2006:427), but does he? And if so, how, and what is he communicating beyond the natural revelation which the apostle Paul deemed sufficient to hold people culpable but not to save them? Not much, if Paul is to be believed (Rom. 10:13-15).

6.7. *Missio Dei*'s "creation mandate" distorts the foundation for mission

We have seen how *missio Dei* places great emphasis on the "creation mandate". But is creation really so wonderful and good? Is it not groaning under a curse?

The Bible does not teach that man is valuable in God's eyes and an object of redemption because he is part of a creation which God is in the process of redeeming. In fact, its teachings "seems to move in the opposite direction. Priority in both curse and redemption lies on humans, not creation" (DeYoung and Gilbert 2011:70).

When Adam ate from the Tree of the Knowledge of Good and Evil he rebelled against God, as a result of which the legal and moral relationship between creator and steward, between king and vassal was broken. This was, indeed, a radical fracturing of relationships, one which had enormous legal consequences, ranging from alienation from God and human suffering to the cursing of the ground (Gen. 3:17), and from which it will not be set free until mankind itself is redeemed from the curse at Christ's second coming.

> When God exiled Adam from Eden, it is not with a commission to continue the work of building the world into a God-glorifying, cultivated paradise. Adam's existence in the world would not be one of continual progress anymore; it would be one of frustration and painful work in a world that was reluctant and even hostile toward him. No, the work of fixing the disaster fell to another, the Offspring of the woman who would crush the Serpent's head... There is nothing in the early chapters of Genesis that would lead us to believe that the work of returning the world to its original 'good state' falls to Adam. God does not give him such a charge, and the reason is that Adam has already blown it (DeYoung and Gilbert 2011:75).

This *missio Dei* fails to recognize. By tying mission to creation it basically bypasses the fall (in spite of lip service to the contrary), which sets it up to cast missions in the wholistic way it does.

> The promised Kingdom of God cannot yet be fully realized under the conditions of fallen creation... This tendency [to try and realize God's kingdom on earth] was bound to lead to a cooling off of evangelistic zeal. Today, evangelical missions are in the same danger if they embrace programmes which are called 'holistic', 'incarnatory' or... 'transforming' mission. Here the concerns for the physical and social well-being of man threaten to outshine eternal salvation (Beyerhaus 2013:9).

The restoration of which the prophets and apostles speak will, indeed, take place—but not until Christ's return. Until Christ comes back we continue to live in "the Noahic version of the cultural mandate. Childbirth still involves pain, work still involves sweat, the animals still run from us in fear, and the creation is still subjected to frustration" (DeYoung and Gilbert 2011:213).

The other misleading implication which *missio Dei* extrapolates from creation is that God can communicate with anyone, anywhere, without prior mediation or spiritual transformation. Now it may be true that God can communicate with anyone, but that truth must be balanced with the other Biblical fact that the natural man is deaf to God's call, and the fact that, as already noted, natural revelation does not provide sufficient information to lead someone to a saving knowledge of Jesus Christ.

6.8. *Missio Dei*'s politicized approach to social transformation is flawed

There are several problems with *missio Dei*'s politicized approach to social transformation. First of all, the biblical concept of justice is not necessarily that which we believe to be the right thing. "The minute one begins to define social justice, one runs into embarrassing intellectual difficulties. It becomes, most often, a term of art whose operational meaning is, 'we need a law against that'" (DeYoung & Gilbert 2011:176, 180). This kind of "mission" can easily degenerate into political lobbying for our favorite causes. There is nothing wrong with individual Christians lobbying for particular causes they feel strongly about, but nowhere does the New Testament tie that to the church's mission.

Secondly, social transformation presents a false hope as the end-goal of the missionary enterprise.

> Many church leaders are doing their people a disservice by leading them to hope too much for the betterment of society 'in this present evil age', which still languishes in bondage and futility. Mission statements like "Transform the City and the World" and "Change the City, Change the World" express a commendable desire, but simply go too far beyond what the Bible tells us we should expect to see in the world during this age, before Jesus returns. And the result, we fear, is that over the years, as cities don't become havens of virtue and justice, as poverty persists, as inadequate housing remains, as governments remain susceptible to corruption, Christians will find themselves discouraged and possibly even questioning the goodness and power of God—all because they have their hopes set too high and on the wrong things (DeYoung & Gilbert 2011:130).

Major aspects of *missio Dei*—everything to do with social transformation—simply don't work in the increasingly large sections of the world where Christians are persecuted, where hope for a better life is firmly wedded to Christ's second coming, where Christians recognize that things will, in fact, go from bad to worse. As Beyerhaus points out, in *missio Dei*

> the 'eschatological realism' of the Bible is being overlooked, i.e. the prophecies about concrete events to be expected to happen at the end of times: the maturation of evil, the empire of the Antichrist, the end of this world and the Last Judgement. If all this is changed into this-worldly programs, then the church is deprived of her chief missionary task of proclaiming the Gospel to those who are far from Christ (Beyerhaus 2013:7).

Thirdly, different Christian denominations have radically different socio-political agendas. In James Davison Hunter's extensive critique of this misguided focus, *To Change the World: The Irony, Tragedy & Possibility of Christianity in the Late Modern World*, he traces and evaluates the very different (almost polar opposite) socio-political agendas of, respectively, the Christian Right, the Christian Left, and the neo-Anabaptists. In broad strokes he summarizes the three positions as follows:

> Among most theological conservatives, the main challenge presented by the modern world has been secularity. Their solution, therefore, is a "resacralization" of society—bringing God back into all spheres of social activity. Among most theological and political progressives, the primary challenge has long been one of inequality, a problem that has grown global over the last two centuries as the disparities of wealth and power in capitalism have grown and internationalized. For progressives, then, the solution is a redistribution of wealth and power with a preference for the poor and needy. Among many neo-Anabaptists, the most significant challenge of our time is the violence and coercion built into the polity of liberal democracy and consumerism of global capitalism. Their solution, then, is the peace-living *koinonia* of the church-based community (italics in original, Hunter 2010:199)

Missio Dei proponents tend to support issues which have a distinctly "progressive/Christian left" flavor. Somehow their exegesis and wholistic views lead to politically correct positions (from a western, progressive point of view) on the issues of the day. It also reflects a profound naivety on how societal change is actually effected.[7]

Hunter argues eloquently that even though "the dominant public witness of the Christian churches in America since the 1980s has been a political witness" (Hunter 2010:12), that political engagement, whether as conservatives or as progressives, has had a very adverse effect on its testimony: "contemporary Christian understanding of power and politics are a very large part of what has made contemporary Christianity in America appalling, irrelevant, and ineffective—part and parcel of the worst elements of our late-modern culture today, rather than a healthy alternative to it" (Hunter 2010:95).

History has shown time and again that a Christian influence that has a tangential relationship to the Church does not generally

[7] I highly recommend Hunter's book to those wishing to delve deeper into the subject of how to effect societal change.

maintain itself as an ongoing Christian witness. It is, in fact, remarkable how rapidly formerly "wholistic" Christian missionary enterprises such as medical, educational and developmental institutions drift from the Christian fold.[8]

♦ ♦ ♦

In the New Testament the term *metamorphoo* [change/transformation] does not refer to social change but to the change which has occurred in those who have been "born again", or transformed by the work of the indwelling Holy Spirit who then begins a work of sanctification in them (Mat. 17:2; Rom. 12:2; 2 Cor. 3:18). This leads them to do all kinds of good works, both corporately and individually:

> Christian missionaries of all denominations have achieved outstanding results in Africa and Asia in the fields of education, medical care and economic development. They produced fruit also by remarkable social improvements, right up to the ordering of state structures. Yet for all of them the desire to call people to conversion and faith in the gospel, and opening for them the way to eternal life, was their first priority. Therefore we, too, in our missionary work, must never neglect the most important gift that we as messengers of Jesus have to bring to all men: the offer of reconciliation with God on the basis of the atoning death of Jesus on the cross and the assurance of eternal life through His resurrection from the dead (Beyerhaus 2013:8).

The political agitation which the proponents of *missio Dei* advocate is very different from the "good works" which missionaries have always sought to do, as well as from the missionary movement we read about in the book of Acts which, more than any other Bible book, paints a picture of the early church's actual missionary enterprise: "If you are looking for a picture of the early church giving itself to creation care, plans for societal renewal, and strategies to serve the community in Jesus' name, you won't find them in Acts. But if you are looking for preaching, teaching and the centrality of the Word, this is your book" (DeYoung & Gilbert 2011:49).

---

[8] For an extensive history of this fact with respect to the Middle East, see my book *Protestant Missionaries to the Middle East: Ambassadors of Christ or Culture?*

They also appointed deacons so that the apostles could devote themselves to the word of God and prayer and, later, elders to "direct the affairs of the church well" (Acts 14:23; 1 Tim. 5:17).

6.9. *Missio Dei* uses questionable exegesis to build a hermeneutic to undergird its vision of mission

Long ago Glasser and McGavran warned presciently against the "new hermeneutic" which would undermine the traditional missionary enterprise in which "a mere reiteration of the words of Holy Scripture would be a betrayal of the gospel" (Glasser & McGavran 1983:98). As we saw in chapter 4, since then at least four different types of missional hermeneutics have evolved. We here focus on the one which presents Old Testament events as paradigmatic (as opposes to merely illustrative) for Christian missions.

The problem with basing a Christian theology primarily on Old Testament paradigms is that it leads to distortions because it does not do justice to the fact that the Bible is a progressive revelation leading inexorably to the crucifixion and resurrection of Jesus Christ, which is the apex of the four gospels and the source from which the subsequent books of the New Testament draws. Wright recognizes that his hermeneutical framework introduces distortions but appeals that we evaluate his model on its "heuristic fruitfulness" (Wright 2006:68). Now it is true that any interpretation of the Bible risks introducing distortions. However, the point of good hermeneutics is to minimize distortions, not introduce them in order to lead the reader to that which the interpreter seeks to communicate!

Bosch dismisses the idea of careful grammatico-contextual exegesis which, as we have seen, is "mere proof-texting" in his eyes. Suddenly the traditional, systematic and exegetical approach to Scripture is perceived as woefully inadequate. He maintains that the contribution of "such elaborate exegesis… towards establishing the validity of the missionary mandate is minimal" (Bosch 1993:439). If he were to be believed then "if we discover in the Bible nothing but 'eternal, immutable truths', the missionary dimension will be quickly dissipated" (:439, 444).

Lastly, creating a hermeneutic after the construction of the praxis also, inevitably, creates distortions. It is like building the foundation after the superstructure has been erected: the foundation is forced into a certain shape because of the pattern above it. Little wonder we see suitably chosen Old Testament events presented as paradigmatic while other teachings and events (like Noah's flood, the extermination of the Canaanites, etc.) are pointedly ignored or reinterpreted in ways that the New Testament writers could not have imagined.

7

If not *Missio Dei*, then What?

♦ ♦ ♦

There is no point in being critical of something if one has nothing constructive to offer in its place. So, if the concept of *missio Dei* as commonly understood today is not the framework within which the missionary enterprise should be conceptualized, what is? This final chapter sketches the contours of an alternative basis for Christian missions. It is essentially a restatement of the view which has informed, shaped and driven missions for a long time, but phrased against the background of the concerns raised in the previous chapters.

The criteria of this alternative paradigm of missions is that it must be clearly rooted in the apostle Paul's teachings and precedent, be church-based and church-focused, and be recognized as truly Christian by fellow Christians from any country—democratic or otherwise—and of any race, any culture or any economic background. Being perceived as truly Christian means it must clash at a theological level with the prevailing culture and must seek to present its message in culturally acceptable ways. In other words, it cannot avoid certain frictions at a civilizational and theological level with the prevailing culture. By its alternative way of life as a Christian community it must present a counterculture with an alternative set of values which stands in quiet condemnation to the dominant worldviews, whether that be ultra-nationalism, untrammeled materialism, state-sponsored terrorism, Islamic extremism or any of a host of other ideologies,

Before spelling out what this looks like we first need to dismiss the idea of a missional hermeneutic, as well as to define some key terms.

7.1. There is no such thing as an overriding missional hermeneutic

As seen in the previous chapter, the proponents of *missio Dei* find the salvation-of-the-soul, Christian discipleship, church-planting model of missions as hermeneutically simplistic, and propose an elaborate, alternative missional hermeneutic in its place. Our response is that there is no such thing as a missional hermeneutic. There is, most certainly, a strong biblical basis and mandate for missions which consists of numerous commands and examples. This is, however, very different from seeing such events as creation, the calling of Abraham, the year of Jubilee, etc, as paradigmatic, as lenses through which we should seek to understand the underlying meaning of the biblical text.

It could be argued, in fact, that any hermeneutic with a self-limiting adjective before it ("allegorical hermeneutic", "liberationist hermeneutic", "feminist hermeneutic", "structural hermeneutic", "demythologizing hermeneutic" "post-structural hermeneutic", etc.) is bound to lead to distortions—and a missional hermeneutic is no exception. In fact, they are a dangerous cycle: just as, say, particular feminist concerns (however valid) create a particular feminist hermeneutic which supports a particular feminist interpretation of the text, so particular missionary concerns (however valid) create a particular missional hermeneutic which supports a particular missional interpretation of the text which, in this case, undergirds the model of *missio Dei*.

Historically, theologically conservative Christians have generally operated from the presupposition that the covenant-keeping, holy and gracious God of the Bible is working out his plan of salvation in the course of human history. At specific times in his systematic, progressive outworking of that plan he inspired people (the Bible's writers) to communicate specific messages with respect to how the covenant community he was calling into being should relate to him, to each other and to the rest of the world. These communications were, by and large, easily understood by the original recipients (the exception being prophetic writings the implications of which only became clear in time). In spite of our cultural, historical and linguistic distance from the original recipients, it is quite possible for the Christian to recapture the essence of their messages—after all, many a person has come to faith simply by reading the Gospel of John or particular sections of Romans. Using such obvious principles of interpretation as the recognition of literary genre, grasping something of the text's historical-cultural and contextual setting and, at times, doing word studies or syntactical analysis—i.e., the kind of stuff you learn at a good Bible school—most of the rest of the Bible becomes quite intelligible. Yes, at times we are left with loose ends, but these are not of such a nature that we cannot know in large measure what God wants us to believe about Himself and how he wants us to behave without having to create a specialized hermeneutic.

The bulk of the historical narratives of the Old Testament illustrate the basic parameters and commands which were embraced (or ignored or neglected!) by the covenant community in the course of its history, and go on to describe the results of that obedience or disobedience. This means that, *with respect to Christian mission theology, events and divine acts described in the Old Testament (such as, say, the exodus), may be illustrative of the parameters set for it in the New Testament, but they are not paradigmatic.* If this be the case then the whole idea of a Christian missional hermeneutic based in large part on Old Testament paradigms is not feasible.

7.2. "Missions", "kingdom of God", "common and salvific grace" defined

Most Protestant Christians of past centuries will, I think, concur with the following definition:

Mission is the church's God-given, Holy Spirit-empowered task to so present the person of Jesus Christ to those unreached with the Gospel that they face a solemn, personal decision to accept or reject Him as their Lord and Savior, to disciple new believers by teaching and modeling Christian truth and values, and to plant local churches according to the New Testament pattern so that believers are established in the teachings of the Christian Scriptures, develop Christian graces, and become equipped to minister to each other and to witness to society (Pikkert 2008:190).

This definition incorporates the Trinitarian nature of missions, the evangelistic emphasis on the free offer of grace and the need for a personal decision, the importance accorded to a transformed life, the focus on establishing local churches, and the obligation that the covenant community has to model Christian values. It is not based on an overarching missional hermeneutic but simply on the church setting out to "do all that Christ commanded them to do" (Mat. 28:20), as interpreted to the church by his apostles.

We define the phrase "the kingdom of God" as *wherever God's rule is gladly embraced.* As such it exists in greater or lesser degrees in the hearts of individuals, collectively in God's covenant communities (whether ancient Israel in the past, or the church today), and to a degree even in the world at large, depending on the extent to which the values a particular society espouses are aligned with those of God. God's kingdom, by this definition, can wax and wane depending on how people respond to God's grace, whether that be his common grace working in society at large or his salvific grace leading people to salvation from the penalty, power and, eventually, the presence of sin. It will reach its permanent apogee at Christ's second coming, when he "will proclaim peace to the nations. His rule will extend from sea to sea and from the River to the ends of the earth" (Zech. 9:10).

Note the distinction in the prededing paragraph between God's common and salvific grace. Common grace consists of the many blessings God bestows on mankind which do not pertain directly to salvation. It exists simply because God is a good God (Ps. 145:9; Mat. 5:45, Acts 14:17, James 1:17). When God withdraws it (as happens at times) there is a rapid deterioration of public order and quality of life. Without it the world would be little different from hell. Thanks to God's common grace, however, there is much that is good, beautiful and uplifting in the world. Most people can appreciate the beauty and harmony of creation. Some have the ability to create works of great beauty in the fine arts, music or architecture or have developed skills with respect to their jobs from which they receive pleasure. The advances in the physical sciences which have made life more comfortable for most testify to God's common grace, as does the fact that most people possess a sense of morality and decency, and seek to love and take care of their families, and protect human life. Some seek the greater good, sometimes at great personal sacrifice. Such things as good government, educational institutions, medical care, charitable organizations and caring communities, as well as environmental concern, all testify to God's common grace. Christians often (and, in fact, should) serve shoulder-to-shoulder with non-Christians in these areas.

Salvific grace is more specific: it pertains to everything God does to draw people into a living, personal relationship with Himself on the basis of the salvation He effected through the person and work of Jesus Christ. The distinction matters because the specific ministry of the church, as a body, should be focused on the realm of God's salvific grace. This is the arena of the Church. Its essential mission is not partnering with God in the reshaping of the world. It is much more specific: it must proclaim the gospel of God's grace in Jesus Christ, disciple those who respond to the gospel call and gather them into church communities who worship God "in spirit and in truth" (John 4:24).

7.3. The role of the church in Christian missions is central

As just pointed out, God's agent in the realm of His salvific grace is the church. Put another way, God specifically ordained and equipped the church—and only the church—for the task of Christian missions. Only the church, and not various and sundry parachurch ministries, is uniquely equipped for the task of fulfilling the Great Commission. Missions is "a law that expressed the nature and that governs the life of the church" (Boer 1975:217) and, as such, cannot be replicated by or ceded to other institutions without it losing its essential character.

This means that the church's mission is much more specific than the way Christians are to live their daily lives. The specific mission of the church is to go to the four corners of the world to declare the gospel of God's redeeming grace in Jesus Christ, disciple new believers, and gather them into churches where they worship Jesus Christ and obey all he commanded but—and this is important—not every command of Christ nor everything Christians do is part of the church's mission.

Christians are not supposed to beat their spouses or commit adultery, but they are to take care of their parents and discipline their children. Christians should be concerned about the environment. Some agitate for affordable housing, others are actively involved in the fight against the exploitation of women and children. In other words, Christians play a role in the realm of God's common grace. However, "there is a difference between the individual Christian and the local church, and therefore we can't just say that whatever we see commanded of the individual Christian is also commanded of the local church" (DeYoung & Gilbert 2006:233).

> It is to this body (i.e., the church) that the Holy Spirit poured out at Pentecost has been given. *He was poured out on the apostles and on the disciples who stood under the spiritual authority of the apostles.* Through the witness of the apostles, through the witness of men appointed by the apostles, and through the

> witness recognized by the apostles, the Church expanded. Because the Spirit indwells the Church, the Church is a witnessing Church. Because He indwells the Church, he indwells every member of the Church, whether officially and corporately through the offices of the institute or through her members personally and individually (italics added, Boer 1975:213).

Boer makes the point that the underlying reason for the missiological failure of past efforts to educate and heal is because, ultimately, educating and healing are part of the created order, social phenomena which occur in one shape or form in all cultures or, as we put it, in the realm of common grace. The church, on the other hand, is the one institution which arises out of the redemptive as opposed to the created order. It belongs to the realm of salvific, not common grace. As such, "it is not her function to educate, or to farm, or to heal, or to pursue scientific investigations. The Spirit that is in her is a Spirit expressing Himself exclusively in witness and in life" (Boer 1975:231). The gospel is the power of God unto salvation (Romans 1:16), and God has entrusted the preaching and communication of that gospel-unto-salvation to the church, whose members are counted a "chosen people, a royal priesthood, a holy nation, a people belonging to God" for the purpose of "declaring the praises of Him who called them out of darkness into his wonderful light" (1 Peter 2:9). If the church doesn't do these things no one else will. It is the church's unique mandate to send out ambassadors who can preach, exemplify core Christian truths, and who strive to create loving and well-taught New Testament-like churches among ethnic groups where there are, as yet, few, if any, such entities.

Furthermore, missionaries are not free to choose whatever they think may lead to the desired end. God has given specific 'marching orders' to the church with respect to its interaction with the world. In other words, Christian missions does, in fact, consist of the church's faithful obedience to those 'militaristic commands' in the New Testament, the idea of which major proponents of *missio Dei* find so passé.

7.4. Some New Testament missionary commands

Before we look at a number of these commands it is only fair to note that, with the exception of the paragraph about letting Paul interpret Christ for us, I don't think the theologically conservative missiologists considered in this book would have trouble accepting the contents of the following points. They would, however, take issue with the fact that they are framed as commands which limit the scope of the church's missionary enterprise.

7.4.1. Let the apostle Paul interpret Christ for you

"*Follow my example me as I follow the example of Christ*" (1 Cor. 11:1).
"*Whatever you have learned or received or heard from me, or seen in me—put it into practice. And the God of peace will be with you*" (Phil. 4:9).

Instead of taking Jesus Christ as their model for missionary praxis, previous generations of missionaries recognized that Paul, in particular, serves as a better model. This is called the representationalist model of missions. In contradistinction to the incarnational model of *missio Dei*'s use of Jesus as the 'prototype', representationalists take the ministry of Paul as an ambassador of Christ, as an evangelist and as a church planter to be the typical pattern or, in some cases, even as the defining paradigm for Christian missions.

Interestingly, on five different occasions Paul himself presents his own life and/or ministry as a model for others to follow (1 Cor. 4:16; 9:22; 11:1; Phil. 3:17; 1 Thes. 1:6). What did that life look like?

> From the moment of his conversion, Paul understood the proclamation of the gospel of Jesus Christ to be his mission in life. But he was more than an itinerant evangelist. His aim was to bring the Gentiles to the obedience of faith (Rom. 1:5) and to organize his converts into self-governing churches. Paul energetically labored not to gain large numbers of converts but to present each person mature in Christ (Col. 1:28-29). Such maturity in the corporate congregation of believers is attained as each one exercises his or her gifts to the edification of the whole (Eph. 4:11-16). In short, Paul was a pioneering, church-planting evangelist (Howell, quoted in Hesselgrave 2005:154).

How did he go about doing this? In his classic *Missionary Methods: St. Paul's or Ours?* Roland Allan states that "the secret of the apostle's success in founding churches lay in the observance of principles which we can reduce to rules of practice" (Allan 1962:151). He describes these as intelligible teaching, manageable organization of the community of believers under local leaders, finances arranged so that the local church can manage independent of outside help, clear teaching about the Christian life and the responsibility Christians have for each other, the responsibility of the local church to administer the sacraments, discipline it members and train leaders, and recognizing the right of the local church to exercise each of the gifts of the spirit (Allan 1962:151-152).

Put another way, the nature of Paul's missionary enterprise consisted of preaching the good news widely and indiscriminately, encouraging new believers, appointing elders, and writing letters to the newly established churches about the meaning of what had happened to them when they accepted Christ as Lord and Saviour, and the impact that should have on their daily lives. In short, Paul's ministry consisted of establishing local churches among the nations who would model the obedience of faith. Once he had done that he could declare about large tracts of the ever trouble-filled Balkans that "I no longer have any room for work in these regions" (Rom. 15:23).

Most of the rest of this chapter merely elaborates some of these Pauline rules of practise.

7.4.2. Proclaim the Gospel clearly

> "*Proclaim the mystery of Christ...*
> *pray that I may proclaim it clearly, as I should*" (Col. 4:3,4).

Evangelism, the proclamation of the gospel of God's grace, is foundational. After all, people, not their societies, are eternal. As C.S. Lewis strikingly pointed out, "nations, cultures, arts, civilizations—these are mortal, and their life is to ours as the life of a gnat. But it is immortals who we joke with, work with, marry, snub and exploit—immortal horrors or everlasting splendors" (Lewis 1973:15).

For proclamation to be effective missionaries must, first and foremost, have clear-cut convictions about the gospel message itself. What they present must be "in accord with sound doctrine" (Titus 2:1). Its essentials and its implications must be firmly etched on their minds and hearts. They must be able to communicate these gospel essentials clearly and, usually, they must be able to do so in a foreign language and cultural framework. This means a lifelong commitment to mastering the local language and becoming bicultural, yet all the while staying within the parameters of New Testament spirituality.

The undoubtedly well-intentioned trend towards contextualizing the Christian message and worship forms into local molds *in order to make them more socially acceptable* runs the risk of fudging foundational truths simply because they are perceived as abhorrent to the host community. Bible translation projects which obscure fundamental concepts, such as the divine sonship of Christ, or the merging of the four gospels into one, or the retranslation of Christian prayer and worship into, say, Muslim forms are not helpful. Examples of the latter are efforts to incorporate the Muslim prayer ritual in Christian worship, dispensing with communal singing and extemporaneous, public prayer in order to make services more palatable to Muslims. If Muslims know anything about Christianity from, say, their own media, they know it believes in the deity of Christ, that there are four gospels, that we don't wash every time before we pray, and that Christian worship involves communal singing.

> Many contextual theologians risk losing sight of the universal truths in the Scriptures. The goal of contextualization is not to create a new God, a new soteriology or a new gospel message. Rather it is simply to understand, teach, live and express the gospel in a way that is relevant to a particular context (Meral EMQ 2005:212).

Presenting the truth with cultural sensitivity, disassociated from obnoxious western cultural practices yet without sliding into syncretism may seem like a tall order. However, small steps at a grassroots level can make a big difference. One effective, Christ-sanctioned way of communicating gospel truths is through the use of parables and stories. Or missionaries might, for instance, resist translating their own choruses and hymns into national languages and have trained ethnomusicologists sift through local music to find forms of prose and poetry to convey fundamental Christian truths (c.f. Blincoe 1998:216). In any case the core truths of the gospel must be clearly presented, taught, shared, gossiped… and lived in a way that is "imitatable" by the host community.

7.4.3. Live a transformed, 'imitatable' life consistent with the message preached

"*Live a life worthy of the calling you have received*" (Eph. 4:1).

Christians are called to be recreated into Christ's image (Rom. 8:29; 2 Cor. 3:18; Col. 3:10). In Christ we see what it means to live in the fullness of the Spirit. In Him we see what a human being can look like whose life fully displays the fruit of the Spirit: love, joy, peace, patience, kindness, goodness, faithfulness, gentleness and self-control. This is what he wants for people, and this is what his specific instructions to his disciples were all about: they were to bear witness to everything he had taught and accomplished through his death and resurrection. They were to be heralds of the gospel of God's saving power and life-transforming grace in Jesus Christ—not "little Christs" themselves in terms of the nature of their ministry. What is written or preached is of little import if it is not first lived in such a way that the lives we live are within reach of the to whom we minister people. Missionary lifestyles must be 'imitatable' in the sense that people who come to faith should be able to realistically hope that, one day, their lives are not hugely different from that of the Christians living among them.

Much of this imitatability takes place at the down-to-earth level of home life which, in other cultures, is often very traditional. For instance, Mallouhi describes the ideal Arab family life as one in which "the husband/father is respected, gender-associated roles are distinct, women are modest, children are obedient… [yet] the wife is valued for herself, not just as a mother, and… is treated with respect by her husband and children" (Mallouhi 1997:103). This kind of cultural adaption does not come easily to the project-orientated, rights-conscious Westerner. The ability to 'live the gospel' contextually and imitatably involves a lifelong process of adopting the positive and neutral cultural values of the host society, particularly with respect to the importance it places on issues such as appearances, hospitality, and family relationships. The notion that the church should play a socially progressive role in society in order to bring it up to western standards has consistently proven to be counterproductive.[9]

The outsider who loves and understands is rare enough to be noticed. This writer, who has spent much of his adult life in the Middle East, can testify that people notice and evaluate everything, down to the smallest detail of the foreigners' home life and family dynamics. This reality presents a great opportunity, for people's acceptance or rejection of any invitation to visit your home or church is largely based upon this evaluation; the book is judged by its covers. Hence spiritual values must not just be taught but also be demonstrated in ways understood by one's neighbours.

---

[9] With respect to the Middle East, see my book *Protestant Missionaries to the Middle East: Ambassadors of Christ or Culture.*

7.4.4. Focus on building up a local church

"Excel in gifts that build up the church" (1 Cor. 14:12).

The pattern of church growth in the New Testament is simple: "the Church grew by the addition of converts to existing congregations and by the organization of converts into new and fully independent congregations" (Boer 1975:221). The importance of establishing such congregations of believers is paramount. Any ministry which does not seek to draw new converts into fellowship with the children of God must be eschewed. Yet missionaries often struggle to develop loving, caring, local, New Testament-style churches characterized by regular times of communal prayer, worship, teaching, participation in the sacraments, and the disciplining of members. Reasons for this failure include linguistic inability, an orientation towards "wholistic" ministries aimed at some real or perceived social evil, an inability to incorporate simple cultural norms into daily life, the fear of being taken advantage of and incorrigible western individualism (Borthwick 2003:436). Yet the importance of such local bodies of believers cannot be overstated, both in terms of proclaiming and in terms of incarnating Biblical truths. New believers need the caring support of a group of people who have also experienced some of the intimidation, threats, ostracism and even physical danger in order to stand firm in the faith (see Johnstone 2001:45). Bosch is absolutely right when he points out that "in a very real sense mission, in Paul's understanding, is saying to people from all backgrounds, 'Welcome to the new community, in which all are members of one family and bound together by love" (Bosch 2003:168). That, at the very least and if at all possible, means having a public profile as a distinctly Christian community of believers.

7.4.5. Expect opposition

""I want you to know, brothers and sisters, that what has happened to me has actually served to advance the gospel" (Phil. 1:12).

The New Testament certainly emphasizes the reality of suffering for the sake of Christ and the gospel. The main connection between missions and suffering in the New Testament is that those who take God's missionary commands seriously may be sure of accompanying difficulty and suffering in a world which rejected Christ and where Satan is active: "If they persecuted me they will persecute you also..." (John 15:16-16:2). This is what Paul refers to when he lists all the things he suffered in the course of his ministry (2 Cor. 11:23-27), when he speaks of "the suffering of Christ flowing over into our lives" (2 Cor. 1:5), of his "participation in Christ's sufferings" (Phil. 3:10-11), of "carrying in our body the death of Christ" (2 Cor. 4:10); of "filling in my flesh what is still lacking in regard to Christ's affliction" (Col. 1:24).

Note, however, that whatever other theological dimensions there may be for suffering (such as discipline or purification), Paul said nothing about the nature of his missionary enterprise as being some kind of "participation with the triune God through the suffering Christ" (Sunquist 2013:173). As the apostle explained to the generation of missionaries he had trained, "suffering for the gospel" is a result of people's negative responses to the proclamation of the gospel message:

> Join with me in suffering for the gospel, by the power of God. He has saved us and called us to a holy life—not because of anything we have done but because of his own purpose and grace… And of this gospel I was appointed a herald and an apostle and a teacher. That is why I am suffering as I am (2 Tim. 1:8, 12).

7.4.6. Disciple, train and relinquish responsibility

"*Go and make disciples*" (Matthew 28:19).
"*Appoint elders in every town*" (Titus 1:5).

From among those who come to faith missionaries must select a few key individuals to disciple if they are to move towards the goal of establishing a church with mature national eldership able to introduce Christianity to society at large. Bosch notes that the apostle Paul didn't "rush breathlessly through the Roman Empire as an announcer of the imminent end of the world" but founded local churches which he nurtured through occasional pastoral visits, lengthy letters, by sending coworkers, by interceding and counseling them on a great variety of practical matters, waiting for them to grow in their spiritual maturity (Bosch 2003:130-131). In other words, the apostle was dedicated to training a mature national leadership, not simply to evangelism, and certainly not to becoming the minister of a congregation himself.

Missions must focus sharply on the discipling of national believers who will give leadership to the indigenous church. Informal but time-consuming one-on-one discipleship and/or more formal training programs must equip potential church leaders for preaching, teaching and counseling. Once again, the importance of modeling these qualities in a way that is imitatable cannot be overstated; theology becomes convincing when it is lived more than when it makes sense.

> Being a theologian means being a teacher whose life is carefully observed. Piety and the intellect are united. Thus theological education... is not simply a transferring of knowledge, but also the emulation of exemplary teachers (Meral 2005:212).

Lastly, authentic church growth and development cannot take place without the eventual transfer of power. Local church leaders must be taken seriously, even if they take the church in directions with which missionaries may be uncomfortable. The missionary attitude should be one of "they must increase, we decrease". Too often, however, western missionaries appear "either unwilling or unable to transfer power to poor third-world peoples" (Bosch 2003:357). Paul was quick to transfer responsibility to local believers, in spite of the risks this entailed. This leads us to our last point.

7.4.7. Trust the Holy Spirit to lead the national church into all truth

"*But when he, the Spirit of truth, comes, he will guide you into all truth*" (John 16:13).

Missionaries must recognize that the same Holy Spirit whom they assume is guiding them is doing the same with national church leaders, who will see things from a different perspective, have had a different history, and who look at reality through the eyes of a different culture. They will, in other words, move in directions foreigners cannot always fully comprehend. It takes a big missionary to work within such a structure, and it takes faith in a big God (Thompson 2002:428).

In short, the input of national converts into how New Testament teachings should be applied at the grassroots level of strategy formulation, along with their involvement in consequent implementation, must be taken seriously. Only then can the missionary "make sure that Christ, not American culture and politics with either its good or its bad points, is our message to a lost world" (McDowel 2004).

The results can be refreshing. National church leadership may, for instance, give a different shape to the formation and teaching of Christian theology. For instance, the Western tradition of isolating theology to the critical detachment of an academic discipline is didactically unacceptable to the Muslim mind:

> Unlike the Western, post-Enlightenment mindset that radically dichotomized the sacred and secular, the Middle Eastern worldview is still open to the interconnectedness of the transcendent and physical worlds—hence its openness to leading and guidance though such phenomena as dreams and visions… Middle Eastern Christians will do theology very different from their counterparts in the West… The Middle Eastern mind is mainly romantic. Knowledge is not processed at the practical level but at the ideological or heart level. This mindset helps to explain, in part, why the Middle East has produced so many suicide bombers. We [Middle Easterners] give our lives to ideologies which speak to our hearts, regardless of the practical consequences. Thus a Middle Eastern theology will be directed primarily at the heart. It will use poetry, heart-felt stories and spiritual reflections. Instead of being systematic, it will be a romantic theology written in the tradition of the *Confessions of St. Augustine*. Systematic dogmatism will have to be replaced with a methodology that is not alien (Meral 2005:212-213).

Note Meral's emphasis on adopting culturally appropriate methods of communicating, not on tweaking the contents of the message to make it less offensive.

7.5. So, what about socio-political involvement?

As seen in chapter 3, proponents of *missio Dei* place great emphasis on the need for the missionary enterprise to become involved in activities leading to social transformation. This has backfired badly in many parts of the world.[10] The missionary taskforce, no matter where its workers originally come from, is too tainted by its own background cultures and prejudices to presume to initiate change on

[10] Once again, with respect to the Middle East, see Pikkert (2008).

social and political issues elsewhere. Their primary task must be to present the gospel of God's grace in Jesus Christ in all its winsomeness, model Christian love and grace on a personal, imitatable level, teach and disciple new believers in core Biblical truths, and draw these individuals into a loving fellowship of believers which, by its countercultural values, will stand in quiet condemnation of the prevailing worldview. However, as the Holy Spirit does His work in the congregation of believers, people will start responding to the needs of their families and local communities. This tends to happen first on an individual basis, then small scale through the local church and, eventually, opportunities emerge for service on a larger scale by means of specialized, organizationally distinct para-church organizations whose successes should also feed into the building up of the church, but whose failures would not directly affect the church's public standing. Let me give a real-life example of how cooperation with major para-church organizations helped build up a small local church.

On August 17, 1999, an earthquake which killed some 17,000 people struck near the city of Izmit, in western Turkey. International evangelical relief agencies moved quickly. In the first days following the quake, the Southern Baptists sent a 10-member disaster relief team along with food, water, and medical supplies, and a mobile field kitchen for one of the tent cities (*Evangelicals React*, WP 1999:3). Numerous other agencies, notably Dorcas Aid, the Netherlands Reformed Church, Operation Mercy, TEAR Fund Netherlands, TEAR Fund UK, World Relief Canada, World Vision Canada, and World Vision USA also provided medical supplies, food, blankets and clothing (*Turkey Earthquake*, WP 2000:7). World Concern and its partnering agencies sent financial aid, food, shelter, and medicine. Operation Mercy sent a team of 14 German, Canadian, American, and Swedish relief workers to give first aid, tents for over 2800 people, food, and clothing to victims (*Evangelicals React*, WP 1999:3).

Good as all these efforts were from a common grace perspective, they could easily have been wasted in terms of building up the local church; their effect might have been on a par with the excellent work done by such secular groups such as Doctors Without Borders (with whom this writer has worked). Fine as their ministrations were, they were not feeding into the arena of salvific grace. However, the very small evangelical Turkish Protestant church demonstrated great initiative. It asked the various Christian relief agencies to serve not under their own banners but under that of the Turkish Protestant

Church. This they graciously did and, as a result, instead of each organization unfurling its own flag to a society which would have no idea who they were, it soon became clear that Christians were ministering very effectively to the victims (*Turkey Earthquake*, WP 2000:7). This turned something which was taking place in the realm of common grace into a Christian missionary event. The expertise of Christian para-church ministries operating together with a wide range of other experts in the broad realm of God's common grace, yet able to do so without losing sight of the fact that, ultimately, the only thing that really matters is the building up of a local church, created "a once-in-a-lifetime opportunity for them [i.e. the Turkish Protestant Church] to gain credibility in the eyes of their predominantly Muslim community" (*Evangelicals React*, WP 1999:3). Indeed, since 1999 the Turkish Protestant Church has become a publicly recognized fact of Turkish life.

The delegation of high-profile social engagement in the area of common grace to specialist para-church organizations which humbly recognize the fundamental significance and centrality of the church as God's agent operating in the ultimately much more important realm of salvific grace, can create a very powerful and comprehensive cycle of grace. When the church focuses on its primary calling of proclamation (whether evangelistically at home or through its missionary enterprise cross-culturally), the teaching of sound doctrine, and discipling new believers, God will grow local churches made up of "born-again" regenerated people. In time these people will serve the church according to their gifts and calling as it carries out its specific ministry within the arena of God's salvific grace while at the same becoming "salt" and "light" to their respective societies as they work together with others for the common good.

Bibliography

♦ ♦ ♦

Allan, R 1962. *Missionary Methods: St. Paul's or Ours?* Grand Rapids, MI: Eerdmans Publishing Co.

Arthur, E 2013. Missio Dei and the Mission of the Church. *The World.* June 2013.

Beyerhaus, PJ 2013. World Evangelization or World Transformation? Tübingen: IKVG/ICV.

Internet April 2015: http://www.ikbg.net/pdf/The-Tuebingen-Call-of-Pentecost-2013-On-Missions.pdf

Boer, HR 1975. *Pentecost and Missions.* Grand Rapids, Michigan: Eerdmans.

Bosch, DJ. 1980. *Witness to the World.* London: Marshall, Morgan & Scott.

Bosch, DJ 1991. *Transforming Mission. Paradigm Shifts in Theology of Mission.* New York: Orbis Books.

Bosch, DJ 10-1993. Hermeneutical principles in the Biblical foundation of mission. *Evangelical Review of Theology*, Vol 17, No. 4.

Brownson, JV 7-1994. Speaking the Truth in Love: Elements of a Missional Hermeneutic. *International Review of Mission*, Vol 83, No. 330.

Castro, E 1993. *The Good News of the Kingdom: Mission Theology for the Third Millennium*, New York: Maryknoll, Orbis Books.

Carson, D. 21/04/2016. Internet: http://www.sermoncentral.com/pastors-preaching-articles/don-carson-how-to-do-justice-and-not-undermine-evangelism-943.asp

Costas, OE 1989. *Liberating News: A Theology of Contextual Evangelization.* Grand Rapids MI: Eerdmans.

DeYoung, K & Gilbert, G 2011. *What is the mission of the church?* Wheaton: Crossway.

Ela, JM 1988. *My Faith as an African.* New York: Orbis Books.

Engelsviken, T 2003. Missio Dei: the understanding and misunderstanding of a theological concept in European churches and missiology. *International Review of Mission* Vol. 92, Issue 367.

Ellwood, RS 2000. *1950: Crossroads of American Religious Life.* Louisville, Kentucky: Westminster John Knox Press.

Esposito, JL 1999. Evangelicals react to Turkey earthquake. *World Pulse.* September 17:13.

Ferdinando, K 2008. Mission: a problem of definition. Themelios 33(1):58.

Glasser, FG & McGavran DA 1983. *Contemporary theologies of mission.* Grand Rapids MI: Baker Book House.

Guder, DL 2000. *The continuing conversion of the church.* Cambridge: Eerdmans.

Guder, DL 2007. *Exhibition of the Kingdom of Heaven to the World.* Louisville: Witherspoon Press.

Hesselgrave, DJ 2005. *Paradigms in Conflict: 10 Key Questions in Christian Missions Today.* Grand Rapids: Kregel.

Hocking, WE 1932. *Rethinking missions: a layman's inquiry after one hundred years.* New York: Harper and Bros.

Hoekendijk, JC 1967. *Kirche und Volk in der deutchen Mission-wissenschaft.* Munich: Chr. Kaiser.

Hunsberger, GR 2011. Proposals for a Missional Hermeneutic: Mapping a Coversation. *Missiology: An International Review.* Vol. 39, No. 3.

Hunter, JD. *To Change the World: The Irony, Tragedy & Possibility of Christianity in the Late Modern World.* Oxford: Oxford University Press.

Johnstone, PJ 1978. *Operation World.* Kent: STL Publications.

Kirk, JA 2000. *What Is Mission? Theological Explorations.* Minneapolis, MN: Fortress Press.

Köstenberger, A 1998. *The Mission of Jesus and the Disciples according to the Fourth Gospel.* Grand Rapids: Eerdmans.

Köstenberger, A & O'Brien P 2001. *Salvation to the ends of the earth: A Biblical theology of mission.* Downers Grove, IL: InterVarsity Press.

Lewis, CS 1973. *The Weight of Glory.* Grand Rapids: Eerdmans.

Mallouhi, C 1997. *Mini-skirts, mothers and Muslims: modelling spiritual values in Muslim culture.* England: Spear Publications.

McGowan, ATB. editor. 2006. *Always Reforming: Explorations in Systematic Theology.* Downers Grove: Intervarsity Press.

Meral, Z 2005. Toward a relevant theology for the Middle East. *Evangelical Missions Quarterly.* April 210-215.

Moltmann, J 1977. *The Church in the Power of the Spirit: A Contribution to Messianic Ecclesiology.* London: SCM Press.

Mott, JR 1924. The outlook in the Moslem world. *The International Review of Missions.* London: Oxford University Press, 321-339.

Newbigin, L 1964. *Trinitarian Faith and Today's Mission.* Richmond, Virginia: John Knox Press.

Newbigin, L 1995. *The open secret: an introduction to the theology of mission.* London: SPCK.

Ott, C 2016. *The Mission of the Church.* Grand Rapids, MI: Baker Academic.

Pikkert, P 2008. *Protestant Missionaries to the Middle East: Ambassadors of Christ or Culture?* Ancaster: Alev Books.

Potter, P 1981. *Life in all its Fullness.* Geneva: WCC.

Richebacher, W 2003. "Missio Dei: the basis of mission theology or a wrong path?" *International Review of Mission*, Vol. 92, Issue 367, p. 588-605.

Rosin, HH 1972. *'MISSIO DEI': an examination of the origin, contents and function of the term in Prostestant missiological discussion.* Leiden, The Netherlands: Interuniversity Institute for Missiological and Ecumenical Research, Department of Missiology.

Samuel, V & Sugden, C. 1999. *Mission as transformation.* Oxford: Regnum.

Shenk, W 1996. *Mission in Bold Humility: David Bosch's Work Considered.* New York: Maryknoll, Orbis Books.

Sider, R 1977. *Evangelism, Salvation and Social Justice.* Bramcote: Grove Books.

Song, CS 1985. *Theology from the Womb of Asia.* New York: Maryknoll.

Smith, WC 1988. Mission, dialogue and God's will for us. *International Review of Mission.* No. 307.

Suess, P 2003. "Missio Dei and the project of Jesus: the poor and the 'other' as mediators of the Kingdom of God and Protagonists of the churches." *International Review of Mission*, Vol. 92, issue 367, p. 560-578.

Sunquist, SW 2013. *Understanding Christian Mission: Participation in Suffering and Glory.* Grand Rapids MI: Baker Academic.

Taylor, JV 1968. *The Uppsala Report 1968.* Geneva: World Council of Churches.

Thomas, NE Editor 1996. *Classic Texts in Mission & World Christianity.* New York: Maryknoll.

Thompson, P 2002. What the 'War on terrorism' is teaching us about missions. *Evangelical Missions Quarterly* October 424-429.

Tiplady, R (ed) 2002. *Postmission: world mission by a postmodern generation.* Carlisle: Paternoster Press.

Turkey Earthquake Update 2000. *World Pulse.* 4 February 7

Vanderwerf, M 2011. 'Missionshift' and the way forward. *Global Missiology* 3(8), 4.

Verkuyl, J 1993. *The Good News of the Kingdom: Mission Theology for the Third Millennium*, New York: Maryknoll, Orbis Books.

Vicedom, GF 1965. *The M ission of God. An Introduction to a Theology of Mission.* St. Louis, Missouri: Concordia Publishing House.

Wright, C 2006. *The Mission of God: Unlocking the Bible's Grand Narrative.* Nottingham: InterVarsity Press.

Wright, C 2010. *The mission of God's people: a biblical theology of the church's mission.* Grand Rapids: Zondervan.

Wright, C 2008. *The God I Don't Understand.* Grand Rapids: Zondervan.

Printed in Great Britain
by Amazon

48227568R00056